Welsh

It's Wales

Place-Names

Unzipped

Brian Davies

SWCH-CAE-RHIW
NO THROUGH ROAD

LLANRHAEADR

GLYN CEIRIOG

RHIWLAS
LLANSILIN
OSWESTRY

y Lolfa

First impression: 2001
Third impression: 2006
© Copyright Brian Davies and Y Lolfa Cyf., 2001

Cover design: Ceri Jones
Cover photograph: Wales Tourist Board

ISBN: 0 86243 514 5

Printed on acid-free and partly recycled paper
and published and bound in Wales by:
Y Lolfa Cyf., Talybont, Ceredigion SY24 5AP
e-mail ylolfa@ylolfa.com
internet http://www.ylolfa.com/
phone +44 (0)1970 832 304
fax 832 782
isdn 832 813

Contents

Acknowledgements

To three people, all fluent Welsh speakers with a passion for their language:

My father, Thomas Davies, who in our walks, fishing trips and drives through Wales took delight in explaining the meanings of the names all round us. It was, in particular, his unzipping and translating of Cwmrhydyceirw, more than fifty years ago, which sparked a lifelong interest in understanding the meanings of names.

My mother-in-law, Elizabeth Ann Griffiths, of Sketty, Swansea, who, later on, willingly took over the role of translator and explainer, particularly relishing the challenges presented by names in south-west Wales, from which her family came.

Marian Davies, of Tycoch, Swansea, a good friend who read early proposals and drafts of *Welsh Place-names Unzipped*, and pointed out several areas where improvements and corrections should be made.

Brian Davies

February 2001

Introduction

Welsh Place-names Unzipped is a unique do-it-yourself handbook for people visiting or living in Wales who cannot speak any Welsh.

With the handbook, you will not only be able to find the meanings of thousands of Welsh city, town, village and countryside names: you will also be able to translate many more thousands of names given to homes, farms, streets, halls of residence and other buildings where people once lived or are still living.

The principles of unzipping and translating Welsh names

Welsh place-names are no different from English names such as Oxford or Newcastle. These city names just run ox and ford, and new and castle together. There is no space between the component words within the names: Oxford and Newcastle are compound – 'zipped-up' – names.

To translate a Welsh place-name you first need to recognize and then unzip the component Welsh words within the compound name.

By using the specially devised word list unique to this translation guide you will, at one and the same time, be able both to recognize and translate those individual word components.

You will soon be delighted to find for yourself that an apparently daunting jumble of letters such as that seen in Tirmynyddteg describes 'A fair mountain land', and that Cwmrhydyceirw is soon unzipped into 'The vale where the stags cross the stream', while Tonypandy describes a long-lost world of lay-lands and woollen workers.

Welsh has the longest literary tradition of any surviving European language, going back to the seventh century AD. As a result, Welsh place-names often give an insight into local history, religion, geography and the natural world.

The pleasure of your time in Wales will be enhanced by making sense of names on signs or maps and in local publications, and you yourself transforming otherwise meaningless letters into vivid, evocative descriptions of where you are, or where you might be heading next.

The Special Welsh Word List simplifies unzipping and translation

This is because:

1   it has been built up using the English, not the Welsh, alphabet.

You can see from page 25 that the Welsh and English alphabets are very different.

One big difference is that the Welsh alphabet has pairs of letters regarded as equivalent to a single letter. Each pair of letters, such as **NG**, **LL**, and **CH** has its own sound.

Another difference is that the Welsh alphabet has no **J**, no **K**, no **Q**, no **V**, no **X** and no **Z**. So if you come across a place-name in Wales with any of these letters in them, you can be certain that it is not a straightforward Welsh form of any name.

Finally, some letters which are only consonants in English are vowels in Welsh: **W** and **Y** are examples.

For a guide to a good approximate pronunciation of Welsh names, please see **A guide to pronunciation of letters of the Welsh alphabet** on pages 26 and 27.

2   it lists variant spellings and historically or grammatically changed forms of Welsh words, just as you find them in place-names: you do not have to worry about word mutations.

The rules of Welsh grammar require the first letters of many Welsh words to change when they follow certain other kinds of words. These first-letter changes are called 'mutations'.

The rules for mutations apply in place-names, too.

If similar rules applied in English place-names, Newcastle on Tyne would have to be written as Newgastle on Dyne, while Melton Mowbrey would become something like Meldon Fowfrey.

A non-Welsh speaker trying to use a standard Welsh dictionary to translate Welsh place-names would be in a double-whammy Catch 22 bind. First, as just discussed, the alphabet is different. Secondly, without knowing the rules for word mutations you wouldn't know in which alphabetical section of the Welsh dictionary to look up the word.

These discouraging Catch 22 complications, which I experienced thirty years ago when beginning to learn Welsh, provided part of the motivation to devise a new kind of word list which, while never being comprehensive, would help to reduce the problems just touched on to an irrelevance.

NB: Readers who would, nevertheless, like some idea of the nature of these word mutations will find more detail in **A summary of the kinds of mutations of Welsh words likely to be found in place-names** on pages 28 and 29.

3   words you are most likely to come across in place-names are set apart from the rest.

There are several words which feature very frequently in Welsh place-names – words such as Llan (the church of), Bryn (a hill), Pentre (a village) and Aber (the outflow of a river).

Out of the Welsh list of about 2,500 words, seventy-five of these most commonly occurring words have been designated as **Key Words**.

Key Words are listed in bold print; they are printed to the left of the main word list and are set apart from adjacent words by spaces above and below their entries.

How to read word entries in the Special Welsh Word List, on pages 10 to 13, shows how the Key Words appear in the list and gives several examples of how to read different kinds of entries in the list.

When you are starting to unzip Welsh place-names it is a good idea to look down the list of Key Words first: you will often find they are all you need to translate the whole name.

In **How to unzip Welsh place-names**, on pages 14 to 18, several examples are given which further illustrate how the word list has been built up.

How to read entries in the Special Welsh Word List

A selection of ten entries which you can find in the Special Welsh Word List follows. Each of the selected entries has been given a reference number. The notes are numbered according to the entry referred to; they explain how to read the word list and show how the list is set out for ease of use.

1	abad -au	abbot
2	abatai/abaty	abbeys/abbey

3 aber the mouth of a river or stream, where it flows into a larger river or into the sea. Nearly always, the name of the out-flowing river follows aber

4	**ap** (before a name)	son of (the named person)
5	âr (1)	ploughed land

6 ar (2) = ar + y on the; upon the; over the

7   ar (3) can mean: opposite; on that side of; nearby

8   **as** (at the end of a plant or tree name) can suggest abundance e.g. Bedwas, from Bedw and as

9 ban -nau -niau -nedd -noedd mountain peak; hill peak

10   **og** (at the end of a word) Like the English -ish, or -ey, or -y, such as in pinkish or milky etc. For example, mawn = peat, so mawnog = peaty

1   abad -au   abbot

abad is the (singular) word which means an abbot; -au means that if you add au to the singular word, abad, you get the plural form for abbots – abadau.

If a plural form is not straightforwardly obtained in this way – i.e. simply by adding letters to the singular form – then the plural form will appear elsewhere in the word list in its own appropriate alphabetic position, with a separate translation.

For example, oen = a lamb, but ŵyn = lambs; one will be found under the **O** section, the other under the **W** section in the word list.

2   abatai/abaty   abbeys/abbey

The forward slash sign between the two Welsh words show (a) that they are closely linked and (b) that the second word would in any case have followed the first in the word list.

The English translation to the left side of the slash (abbeys) applies to the Welsh word to the left of the corresponding slash (abatai); while abbey is the translation of abaty.

3 **aber**   the mouth of a river or
                                                  stream, where it flows into
                                                  a larger river or into the sea.
                                                  Nearly always, the name of
                                                  the out-flowing river follows
                                                  aber

The special nature of this word is shown by (a) the vertical space between it and other entries, (b) its appearance to the left of the majority of entries in the main word list and (c) the use of bold type.

Aber is a Key Word – that is, one of those words which appear very often in Welsh place-names.

When unzipping Welsh names you should first check down the list of these set-apart Key Words. Soon, many of them will become so familiar to you that you'll ignore them and move on to the next word element in a name. Aberystwyth and Aberaeron are examples of words containing aber; the Ystwyth and the Aeron are rivers.

| 4 | **ap** (before a name) | son of (the named person) |

Important prefixes and suffixes – that is, letters which are not words in themselves but come before or after ordinary words to add meaning – appear in bold but, unlike Key Words, they are not set apart in the main word list.

This particular entry tells you that if you put **ap** before the name **Rhys**, say, then ap Rhys means the son of Rhys. The English version of ap Rhys is Preece or Price. In front of a name starting with a vowel, ap changes to ab. Ab Owen became Bowen in English.

| 5 | âr (1) | ploughed land |

| **6 ar (2) = ar + y** | on the; upon the; over the |

| 7 | ar (3) | can mean: opposite; on that side of ; nearby |

5, 6 and 7 all deal with the word (element) ar.

ar (2) is clearly a Key Word, as it is in bold, and is set with space above and below it, and is found to the left of the main word list (see notes on aber, above). So the most likely meaning of ar when you come across it will be 'on the' or 'upon the' or 'over the'.

Alternative translations of **ar (2)** are indicated by means of semi-colons (;) between each of the translations.

With all three versions of ar, the other words in the place-name you are translating will help you to decide which is the more likely meaning of ar in that name.

8	**as** (at the end of a plant or tree name)	can suggest abundance e.g. Bedwas, from Bedw and as

Bedw means a birch tree, and if you add as to it you get Bedwas. It follows that Bedwas means a (place with a) great number of birch trees.

9 ban -nau -niau -nedd -noedd   mountain peak; hill peak

Ban, a mountain peak or a hill peak, is a Key Word chosen here just to illustrate that, like many Welsh words, it has several forms of plural: in this case, bannau, banniau, bannedd, and bannoedd. Multiple forms for the plural of a word are much more common in Welsh than in English.

10	**og** (at the end of a word)	Like the English -ish, or -ey, or -y, such as in pinkish or milky etc. For example, mawn = peat, so mawnog = peaty

The suffix **og** changes a word into an adjective.

How to unzip Welsh place-names

Here are several examples of unzipping place-names to illustrate and clarify the process of translating, using the Special Welsh Word List on pages 34 to 93.

Example 1: Nantyffin

Let's say you want to translate the place-name **Nantyffin**, just seen on a road sign or map.

You don't yet know how many words are zipped up together in that name; and you don't yet know where the first word in the name **Nantyffin** ends. All you know is that the first word starts with **N**.

So you turn to the beginning of the **N** section of the alphabetical word list on pages 79 to 80 and you first check the Key Words, which are those printed in bold type to the left of the other words and in their own clear space. (Please see pages 10 to 13, if you haven't already read **How to read word entries in the Special Welsh Word List.**)

You won't find **n** or **na** or **nan** among the Key Words but you will find **nant**, translated as **stream**. The first word, **nant**, has now been unzipped and translated.

After **nant** comes the letter **y**. Right at the start of the alphabetical **Y** section, you'll see **y** is also a Key Word, meaning **the**, or **of the**. So that's the next step done.

In the **F** section you'll next find **ffin**, and see it means **boundary**, or **a boundary**.

Nantyffin has now been completely unzipped into **nant**, **y**, and **ffin** and been translated into something like 'stream of the boundary', or 'the boundary stream'.

Example 2: Cwmrhydyceirw

As with Nantyffin, you don't yet know how many words are in the name, nor where they start and finish.

So starting in the **C** section of the alphabetical word list, you look first at the Key Words.

You won't find **c** or **cw** among them, but **cwm** is there, so that's now unzipped: it means **valley** or **a valley.**

In the **R** section, **rhyd** will be found as yet another Key Word: it means a **ford**, or **river crossing-place**.

As in Nantyffin, the one letter Key Word **y** comes next, meaning **the** or **of the**.

So three elements in the name have now been sorted. That leaves the letters **ceirw**. There is no helpful Key Word in the **C** section, so you have to look down the rest of the main word list.

There you will find **ceirw** as a single word, meaning **red deer stags**.

So the compound word **Cwmrhydyceirw** has now been split up into **Cwm** and **rhyd** and **y** and **ceirw**: four words.

It can be translated, then, as something like: 'valley of the red stag's crossing', or the very English-sounding 'Stagford Vale'.

Example 3: Tonypandy

A check on the Key Words under the **T** section will find nothing useful.

But in the main word list in the same section you will find **ton**. It can mean one of two things: **ton** (1) means **lay-lands** – i.e. land given over to grass; **ton** (2) means a **wave** (on water). At this stage of unzipping you don't know which is the right **ton**, so just keep them both handy.

Key Word **y**, as in both previous examples, means **the**, or **of the**, and you probably didn't have to bother to look it up this time.

Under **P** in the list there's no useful Key Word. In the main list, though, you'll find **pan** and see it means **fulling** – that is, the process of washing and thickening wool. (If pan is written with an accent – **pân** – it means the fulled cloth.)

Finally in the **D** section you'll see that a meaning of the two letters left – **dy** – is a **house**.

Tonypandy is, then, a four-word name, **Ton** and **y** and **pan** and **dy**:

that is, **lay-lands** and **the/of the** and **fulling** and a **house**. (**ton** (**2**) makes little sense here, of course.)

So putting the four elements of **Tonypandy** together you have a set of words which may reasonably be translated as something like 'lay-lands where there was a house used for fulling' or, perhaps, 'lay lands belonging to the fulling mill'.

Whichever way you choose to translate it, the name tells you of a largely forgotten history of the area around the town.

Example 4: Machynlleth

In the main **M** section, you have a choice of two meanings of **Ma**: the first, **ma** (**I**), is a very old word meaning a **meadow** or a **plain**; **ma** (**2**) means a **place** or a **spot**. So both must be kept in mind, for now.

In the **C** section, **chynlleth** is seen to be modified spelling of a person's name: **Cynllaith**.

(For completeness, this same name, **cynllaith**, could also be the name of a commote, that is, a neighbourhood or locality subordinate to a cantref which, in turn, is similar to the English hundred with its own court of law.)

So **Machynlleth** is a two-word name meaning either 'Cynllaith's meadow', or 'Cynllaith's place/spot'.

The first choice is probably the more likely.

Example 5: Llansaintffraidglynceiriog

In the **L** section, **Llan** will stand out as a Key Word, with a lengthy explanation of its earlier meanings. Probably more Welsh place-names start with **Llan** than any other; it nowadays means **church/the church of**.

Under **S**, you'll find that **saint** – another Key Word – is the same as **saint** in English.

So far, the name deals with a church of some **saint**. Immediately after the word **saint** you can expect the saint's name to follow, and in **F** in the main section, **Ffraid** will be found as **Bride** or **Bridget**.

Glyn, among the **G** section Key Words, means a **glen**, or a **valley**.

Finally, from the **C** section, **ceiriog** emerges as a river name or a person's name. (If a person's name is involved, then this **Ceiriog** was a nineteenth-century poet and farmer, John Ceiriog Hughes, whose middle name was taken from the river Ceiriog.)

Llansaintffraidglynceiriog, then, is a five element place-name combining **the church of** with **Saint** and **Bridget**, and **glen** and **Ceiriog**. So a translation such as 'Saint Bridget's Church in the Glen of Ceiriog' wouldn't be far out.

Example 6: Epynt

This handbook has been written to ensure that English speakers who know no Welsh will be able to make good sense of thousands of Welsh place-names, in a way similar to someone who understands Welsh well but has no specialist knowledge of Welsh words in linguistic and historical settings.

But, as the section '**A final comment about do-it-yourself translations of place-names**…' on pages 32 and 33 makes clear, along with the place-names you will translate with this book there will always be names that, despite your best efforts to unravel them, will remain perplexing. They would be just as puzzling to most Welsh-speaking people too.

The old name **Epynt** seems to me to epitomize such intractable words. It combines severe verbal contractions of two words with a spelling variation in the first.

Because of these difficulties, you'll find **Epynt** explained in full in the main word list.

It was at first, presumably, **Ebynt**, where the **eb** comes from **ebolion**, which means **colts** or **horses**, plus **hynt**, which means **tracks**, or **trails**, or a **way**. Then its spelling changed: the **b** went to a similar sounding **p**.

Epynt, then, means something like **horse trails**.

So, the name **Mynydd Epynt**, where **mynydd** means **mountain**, will mean something like 'the mountain where horses roam'.

Example 7: Dunvant/Dyfnant

Warning bells should be ringing already: there is no **V** in Welsh, as can be seen from the section '**The English and Welsh alphabets compared**' on page 25.

So this 'Welsh' place-name has to be different in some special way from those 'true' Welsh names in Examples 1- 6.

Dunvant is an English corruption of **Dwfn nant**, which you would be able to translate as 'a deep stream', or 'a stream which has deeply cut its own narrow valley'. As a result, **Dunvant** is explained in full in the word list, as are several other examples of names which have crossed language boundaries and whose spelling has become mangled as a result. The language shift might be from Latin to Welsh, Welsh to Saxon, Norman French to English or any other kind of cross-over.

Example 8: all names – and your responsibility

All you have to bring to your translations from time to time is a little imagination of a romantic, Celtic kind, so that you transform a name like **Pontycymer** (which you will quickly unzip into **Pont + y + cymer**) from its brutally basic literal translation of 'Bridge the confluence', into the more charming 'The bridge where two rivers meet'.

I hope you have a lot of pleasure, surprise and delight from using this book.

The history of Wales and Welsh place-names

From the early eighteenth century, as a result of the brilliant ethnological and linguistic researches of Oxford academic Edward Lluyd, the Welsh have been quite proud to see themselves – ourselves – as direct descendants of an ancient continental people. Our Celtic ancestors, way back in the Stone, Bronze and Iron Ages were, of course, successful, cultured, noble and civilized, if necessarily a little belligerent from time to time.

We had been taught that successive waves of our Celtic ancestors spread north and west through Europe from a heartland somewhere near present-day Romania. They crossed the Channel in a succession of conquests. They settled, bringing with them their continental (superior) lifestyles, together with the language, or languages, from which Welsh, Cornish, Breton and Gaelic were later derived.

New discoveries and revised interpretations of archaeological evidence from the centuries before the Roman era are making historians think again. The likely nature of the social and ethnic relationships between the continental Celtic peoples and the established groups of people inhabiting the British Isles is being re-assessed.

The current alternative argument is that there is no evidence of any significant movement of continental Celts crossing into the British Isles in the pre-Christian centuries. What really came across the channel were selectively imported continental goods, tools and implements – along with an increasing awareness of continental ways of life.

About three thousand years ago, the people who imported the goods and artefacts were living in thriving, if smallish, communities across much of Britain. They had well established cultural and social structures, and were involved in planting crops, cultivating woodlands, making pottery and keeping herds of animals. Such communities were not necessarily all of continental Celtic stock; nor was their advancement dependent on an inflow of continental Celtic peoples with more advanced technologies and ways of life.

No one can yet be certain what languages these Bronze and Early Iron Age people spoke.

Later, however, when the Romans came to Britain at the very end of the Middle Iron Age, they reported on the languages they heard among the British tribes and peoples. In summary, the languages or dialects spoken included early forms which would later evolve into Gaelic or Welsh or Cornish. In south Wales, for example, the Silures tribe spoke a language similar to Irish Gaelic; in middle England a different Celtic-type language was in use.

Figure 1 on page 24 gives one modern proposal for the origins of the family of languages spoken in Britain two thousand years ago, and since; but why and when and where these languages first became commonly spoken, and in which parts of the British Isles, is still not really clear.

During the last two thousand years Romans, Angles, Saxons, Normans and the English have been the dominant groups in Britain. The survival or disappearance of pre-Roman languages has depended on the extent to which local populations were, from choice or coercion, affected by and absorbed into the different incoming cultures and ways of life.

It seems that the inhabitants of the easily over-run lowland areas soon became assimilated by the invaders, and so lost their pre-conquest languages. People in the less accessible western hills were not obliged to interact with the same invaders on a similar day-to-day basis.

So geography, as much as anything, seems to have kept the Welsh, Cornish and Gaelic languages alive down through the centuries when successive invaders were extending their influence west and north in Britain.

Wales, as a geographical entity, began to be defined by the Saxons, who built Offa's Dyke to ensure they kept the fertile land to its east for themselves. As a political entity, Wales self-identified after the Normans came, during the wars of the Welsh-speaking princes against the English in the twelfth and thirteenth centuries. Once Welsh resistance had been crushed in the thirteenth century, Wales became a geographically well defined principality administered by the English. Even so, the Welsh kept their language alive in most of Wales, and it always remained strong in the remoter areas.

Place-names in the areas of Wales settled or governed by non-Welsh invaders reflect each and every foreign influence. This is particularly true for place-names all along the more accessible eastern borders of Wales and along the southern coastal corridors. Some examples of Welsh place-names derived from Latin and Anglo Saxon, of English names from Norman French, and cross-combinations of all of these languages can be found in the word list.

After the Romans left, while the Angles and the Saxons were successively causing strife further east, the people in Wales and Ireland had three or four centuries when they were left in comparative peace. Welsh and Irish culture and religion thrived. By the seventh century Welsh was a written language. There were intermittent raids from Viking groups, some of whom had bases in Scotland, but there was no long-term interruption to a life which was becoming increasingly centred on Christianity.

Many Welsh place-names dating from pre-Norman times reflect the central importance of the Church and of its saints and holy people in Welsh life. A majority of names beginning with 'Llan' (the church of) pre-date the Norman Conquest. In the same era, many personal names of revered individuals were changed from their Latin or Saxon forms into Welsh equivalents, and vice-versa, so you may find any of these name forms in Welsh place-names.

Serious invasions and coastal settlement by Vikings came in the ninth and tenth centuries. This is why, on the west and south coasts of Wales you'll find Viking names such as Swansea (from *Sweyn's Ey* = Sweyn's island), islets called *holms*, and The Worm's Head (from early Scandinavian *wyrm*, a dragon – it was the invincible *wyrm* which came in the night that took Beowulf 's life).

The cross-language spelling of personal and place-names, mentioned earlier, continued in later Saxon times and down through the Norman and English centuries. During the industrial revolution, in particular, south and east Wales was settled by many non-Welsh speaking people, which is why so many place-names in those parts are obviously of English origin or are anglicized forms of the original Welsh.

There are two areas of west and south Wales where English place-names predominate for special reasons. The countryside around Tenby has for centuries been called 'Little England beyond Wales'; and in the south of the Gower peninsula, just west of Swansea, there are also very few Welsh place-names.

The reason for the 'Little Englanders' is that in the eleventh century the Normans brought Flemish workers over to the Tenby area to establish wool, wine, fishing and weaving trades.

The workers' loyalty was to their pay-masters, not to the conquered locals. With time, the Flemish communities identified more and more with the Norman English and gave support to them when there was fighting between England and the Welsh princedoms.

By the twelfth century the Gower peninsula was also ruled by the Normans. They built a number of fortifications, some of which were developed by the end of the thirteenth century into the stone castles whose ruins still dominate parts of the landscape. A Gower name like Parc le Breos reminds us that Le Breos was the first Norman overlord of the area, with Swansea the local fortified capital of the region. When the Normans ruled, people from the West Country settled there, practised their open field cultivation system and so helped shape and maintain the non-Welsh characters of both the countryside and the people.

Along with English, Norman, Saxon, Viking and Latin names, Wales also has a number of Hebrew, or biblical, names. Golan, Hebron, Bethlehem, Beulah, Peniel and Bethesda are examples. Such names are evidence of the fervour of the Welsh people during the religious revivals at the end of the nineteenth century.

In Wales, most road signs give place-names in both Welsh and English. The English version is often a useful direct translation of the Welsh original: Bridgend for Penybont, for example. But now and then you'll find no obvious correspondence between a Welsh place-name and the English name provided alongside. This is because both names have been used together down the years by the local inhabitants. Swansea, just mentioned, is a classic example of a city with two entirely separate kinds of name. In Welsh it is called Abertawe (i.e. Mouth of the (river) Tawe); in English it retains the form derived from the (Viking) Sweyn's Island.

Figure I

A recent (1992) proposal for the relationships between Welsh and other Celtic Group languages*

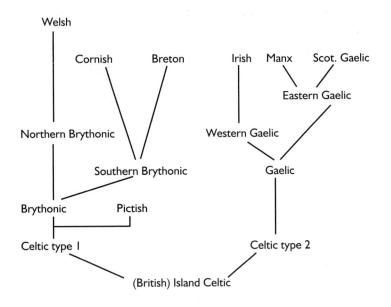

*after *The Celtic Languages*, Cambridge University Press, 1992 (edited by D Macauley)

The English and Welsh alphabets compared

English

A B C D E F G H I J K L M N O P Q R S T U V W X Y Z

Welsh*

A B C CH D DD E F FF G NG H I L LL M N O P PH R RH S T TH U W Y

In the Welsh alphabet, **CH, DD, FF, NG, LL, PH, RH** and **TH** are regarded as being single letters, each with its own pronunciation.

W and **Y** are also vowels.

The Welsh alphabet has no **J,** no **K,** no **Q,** no **V,** no **X,** and no **Z...**

... so, words containing these letters must be non-Welsh, a useful fact to remember when looking at place-names in Wales.

*For a good approximate south-Walian pronunciation of Welsh words, which would be easily understood throughout Wales, please see **A guide to pronunciation of letters of the Welsh alphabet** on pages 26 and 27.

A guide to pronunciation of letters of the Welsh alphabet

Then, that Sunday, the thoughtful cab driver soon found Gary's lemon-coloured jeans floating high up in the wild loch.

This sentence is a mnemonic to Welsh pronunciation.

It contains all the sounds needed for a good approximate south Wales accent, which would be understood all over Wales.

A B C CH D DD E F FF G NG H I L LL M N O P PH R RH S T TH U W Y

Welsh letter	pronounced as
a (short)	a in cab
(with accent)	a in Gary
b	b in cab
c	c in cab
ch	ch in loch (as Scots pronounce it)
d	d in driver
dd	th in then
e (short)	e in then
(longer)	ay in Sunday
f	v in driver
ff	f in thoughtful
g	g in Gary
ng	ng in floating
h	h in high

i (short)	i in in
(longer)	as ea in jeans
l	l in lemon
ll	start as if about to say the l in lemon, then quickly breathe out through the mouth only
m	m in lemon
n	n in lemon
o (short)	o in lemon
(with accent)	oa in floating
p	p in up
ph	f in thoughtful, but stressed
r	r in Gary, but slightly trilled
rh	briefly trilled r, as in Gary, but with brief h as in high, added straight away
s	s in Sunday
t	t in floating
u (short)	i in in
(long)	ea in jeans
w (short)	u in thoughtful
(long)	oo in soon
y (short)	i in in
(long)	ea in jeans
(medium)	u in Sunday

A summary of the kinds of mutations of Welsh words likely to be found in place-names

NB: The book has been written so that you don't have to know anything about mutations of words before you translate place-names.

However, some readers may be interested to know a little about some of the kinds of changes to the beginnings of words – the mutations – which commonly occur.

This section briefly deals only with the kinds of changes of the first letters of words which may be found in place-names: there are, though, other types of mutations in written and spoken Welsh.

No grammatical reasons for the mutations which can occur are given here. Mutations seem to have evolved to make the flow of spoken language easier.

Mutation type 1
NB: These are ones you are likely to find in place-names and in the Special Welsh Word List on pages 34 to 93

This first letter in a word	can change to this	Examples
b	f	bach to fach (small)
c	g	celli to gelli (grove)
d	dd	dafad to ddafad (sheep)
g	-	gwaun to waun (meadow)
ll	l	llyn to lyn (lake)
m	f	melin to felin (mill)
p	b	pen to ben (top of)

rh	r	rhan to ran (piece [of land])
t	d	telyn to delyn (harp)

Mutation type 2

NB: These are found only rarely in place-names, following words such as **fy** (my) and Key Word **ym**, a form of **yn** (in the).

This first letter in a word	can change to this	Examples
b	m	buallt to muallt (pasture)
c	ngh	cornel to nghornel (corner)
d	n	dinas to ninas (fort; city)
g	ng	gwaith to ngwaith (work)
p	mh	pont to mhont (bridge)
t	nh	telyn to nhelyn (harp)

Selected references and further reading

I Dictionaries

Pre-eminent are the first three volumes of a scheduled 4-volume dictionary, the mammoth *Geiriadur Prifysgol Cymru* (Dictionary of the University of Wales). The results of a continuing research project which has already taken teams of Welsh scholars fifty years, these word mines are the ideal resource for anyone exploring the meanings of Welsh place-names. This outstanding University of Wales Press publication was the main source relied on whenever there was uncertainty about the translations of words in place-names.

Later editions of *Y Geiriadur Mawr* (The Big Dictionary) were also most useful because they include very old Welsh words, clearly distinguished as being archaic – exactly the kinds of words likely to be found in Welsh place-names, as so many of them have origins going far back in time. *Y Geiriadur Mawr* is published by Gwasg Gomer in two volumes: English to Welsh and Welsh to English.

Among other dictionaries, both *Y Geiriadur Newydd* (The New Welsh Dictionary) published by Christopher Davies, Llandybie, and the Collins-Spurrell Welsh Dictionary, published by Collins, have lists of personal names and names of birds, animals and rivers.

For readers who may be learning Welsh I should like to make a short digression here to mention Heini Gruffudd's recent (1998) *Welsh Learner's Dictionary*, which I have only just come across. It is also published by Y Lolfa. The dictionary necessarily follows the Welsh alphabet for its (modern) word list, but when translating Welsh words and verb forms it lists many of them both in their grammatically correct form and in the forms and spellings which you actually find in speech and print.

2 A few recommended Welsh texts

If you can read Welsh, then any good library will carry or get hold of a number of good, but out of print, books for you. Several of these take a selection of place-names and explore their possible meanings; some deal exclusively with the names in a small region of Wales. Here I just want to mention four books on Welsh place-names which are still available in bookshops and which deal with names across Wales and are full of interest for anyone who enjoys linguistic detective work.

In *Enwau Tir A Gwlad* (Land and country names), Melville Richards takes about ten themes – such as parishes, churches, castles, forts and dwelling places – and travels across Wales looking, in alphabetical order, at hundreds of place-names. The book is published by Gwasg Gwynedd, Caernarfon (1998).

Yn Ei Elfen (In his element), by Bedwyr Lewis Jones (Gwasg Carreg Gwalch, 1992), spends a single page analysing one of more than a hundred place-names considered in the book.

The two volumes of *Ar Draws Gwlad* (Across the land), edited by Gwynedd O Pierce and colleagues (also Gwasg Carreg Gwalch, 1997 and 1999) cover another 120 place-names.

All the above make fascinating reading and, of course, refer you to other publications in Welsh.

A final comment about do-it-yourself translations of place-names, and the objectives of this book

If you took an English place-name, like Cambridge in Gloucestershire, and unzipped this two-part name into Cam and bridge, you would be factually and historically correct to conclude that this Cambridge was where there was a bridge over a river called the Cam. (By the way, 'cam' comes from an old Welsh word meaning crooked or winding, so it's 'the bridge over the winding river', which is more evocative.)

But if you take the name of the university town of Cambridge and unzipped it in the same way, you would be wrong if you came to a similar conclusion about the origins of the name. For whereas Oxford is quite straightforward, as seen in the introductory pages, Cambridge is, well, somewhat backward.

For a start, the significant river in Cambridge is the Granta.

In Bede's time, about 750 AD, the town was Grantacaestir, meaning 'Roman fort on the Granta'. By the thirteenth century it was Grantabruge, or Bridge on the Granta. Under Norman influence the first G of Grantabruge got changed to C and the first r was lost. So Grantabruge became something like Cantabruge – hence MA (Cantab) etc. Then the nta of Cantabruge became an m, leaving Cambrugge, where brugge still meant bridge, and so on to modern Cambridge.

After which, by a not untypical bit of local inverse logic, part of the river Granta flowing through Cambridge was called the Cam.

Linguistic purists may wish to point out that the straightforward approach adopted in this booklet to enable you to unzip and so quickly get to the meanings of Welsh place-names will from time to time mislead you in just such a Cambridge (university) sort of way.

That's quite correct, of course. What is also true is that no book of this kind could ever be comprehensive in its coverage of all Welsh place-names: the number of linguistic variables alone would be too great – and that's before having to take into account the very large number of personal names and their variant spellings. Even fluent Welsh speakers would need expert academic help to unravel those names whose elements have been corrupted over the centuries. (**Epynt** is given as an example of this kind of word in the section **How to unzip Welsh place-names** on pages 14 to 18.)

Nevertheless, what this handbook still makes uniquely possible is quick, easy and reliable access to the proper meanings of thousands of Welsh place-names, allowing readers to translate them just as they would be translated by a fluent Welsh-speaking person who is not a linguistic historian.

And that's what this book sets out to achieve.

Note: For readers who can read Welsh and who would like to read more about the origins and meanings of a large selection of 'difficult' place-names, there is a short list of readily available and very stimulating books in the **Selected references and further reading** section on pages 30 and 31.

The Special Welsh Word List

Please read **How to read entries in the Special Welsh Word List**, on pages 10 to 14.

It must be strongly stressed that the translations given here, while appropriate for the Welsh words found in Welsh place-names, may not be appropriate translations of the same words when they occur in other, more general and more modern contexts.

A

ab (before a name)	son of (the named person); ab comes before names beginning with vowels
abad -au	abbot
abatai/abaty	abbeys/abbey
aber	the mouth of a river or stream, where it flows into a larger river or into the sea. Nearly always, the name of the outflowing river follows the word aber
aberfa -oedd	the place where there is a river outflow
Abergavenny	from Welsh: Aber Gofenny
abon	a person's name
acer -au	acre of land
aches	flood; tide
adar	birds
addef-i	home; dwelling
addien	beautiful; fair
addoldai/addoldy	places/place of worship
aderyn	bird
adran -nau	section (of land)
adwae	mountain passes
adwy -au -ion -on	gap or pass in mountain; can also mean lair; nook
ael -iau	brow (of hill)
aelhaearn	a person's name
aer	air
aeron	berries; fruit; also a river name
aes	shield

aethnen	aspen; also a river name
aethwy	a tribal name
afal	apple
afan	raspberries; a person's name; also a river name
afanen	raspberry
afon -ydd -oedd	river
agen	cleft; fissure
agendor	gulf; abyss
agor	(to) open
aidan	a saint's name
aig	sea
ail	second (adjective)
aithnen	aspen; also a river name
ala	a person's name: Raleigh
alaf (1)	a person's name
alaf (2) -oedd	cattle
alarch -od	swan
aleg	a person's name; (but see Basaleg,too)
allgo	a person's name: Gallgo(f)
ally	a person's name: Alun
allt	wooded slope
aloag	a person's name
alwen	a person's name; also a river name
aman	a river name
amlwg	prominent; famous; also exposed
amroth	a river name (from Irish: *rath* = fort)
andras	a person's name: Andreas, Andrew
angel	angel
angell	a river name
angharad	a person's name
Anglesea	Swedish viking: ?Angle's island
angor -au -ion	anchorage; bay; also bay tree; laurel tree
angylion	angels
anhun	a person's name
ant	a river name
ap (before a name)	son of (the named person)
âr (1)	ploughed land

         on the; upon the; over the

ar (3)	can mean: opposite; on that side of; nearby
aran	a river name
ardal -oedd	district; region; area
ardd	old word for high place/land
arddyn	a person's name; also a river name
ardudwy	from tribal name, Ardud: see wy endings on page 91
aresg	sedges
arfon	from Welsh: ar(3) + Môn (Anglesey)
argae -au	dam
arglwydd -i	lord
argoed -ydd	enclosure of trees; also a river name
arhos -ydd	a stay; to stay
arhosfa	abode; stopping place
arian	silver; money
arlwydd -i	lord
armon	a person's name: Garmon, Germanius
aros -ydd	a wait; a stop; aros also = to wait

arth (1)   (high) land

arth (2)	bear; a person's name: also a river name
arth (3)	hill; enclosure; mountain ridge; uncultivated land (see e.g. Cenarth)
arthur	a person's name: Arthur
artro	a river name
arwystl	a person's name
as (at the end of a plant or tree name)	can suggest abundance: e.g. Bedwas, from Bedw and as (a lot of birches)
asa(f) or asaff	a saint's name: Asaph
asgell	wing
asyn -nod	donkey
aur	gold; golden
awch	edge
awel -oedd -au -on	breeze
awen or awyn -au	bridle; rein
awyr	sky; air

B

babo	a saint's name: Pabo

bach (1) small

bach (2)	corner; nook
bad -au	boat
badarn	a saint's name: Padarn, Paternus
badrig	a saint's name: Padrig, Patrick
bae -au	anchorage; bay; also bay tree; laurel tree
baedd -od	boar
bagillt	from English: Backelie, field of Bagga or Bacga
baglan	small staff/stick; a man's name
bagwy(n) -au -on	tuft; bunch
bala	originally a hill pass; later the exit of a river from a lake

ban -nau -niau -nedd -noedd mountain peak; hill peak

bân	a river name
banadl	broom

banc bank; mound

Banc y Warren	from English: Warren tree (i.e. gallows) hill or, simply, a rabbit warren
bangor -au	monastery; also an upright part of a wattled fence or hedge
bann -au	peak
banwy	a river name
bar (1)	possibly short for barcut = buzzard or kite
bar (2)	a very old word for hilly country
barcud -iaid	kite
barcut	kite or buzzard
barcutan -od	kite
bardd	poet; bard
bargod -ion	border; marches; also a river name
barlad	drake
Barmouth	from/in Welsh: Y Bermo or Abermaw
barred	a person's name: Barret, Barrat
Barry	from Welsh: Y Barri; possibly from old Welsh barren suggesting top of a hill

Basaleg	either from Welsh: Maes Aleg; or more likely from Latin: *basilica*=church
baw	dirt; mine
bawan	a river name
beblig	a person's name: Peblig
bech (with rivers)	small
bechan	small; also a river name
bed (1)(care with bedw)	a dwelling, from bod (prevalent in south Wales in this form)
bed (2)	a saint's name: Pedr, Peter
bedd -au -i	grave
beddrod -au	tomb; grave
bedr	a saint's name: Pedr, Paternus
bedrod -au	tomb; grave
bedw -en	birch tree; a river name
beeg	a river name
beguil	a river name; perhaps corruption of bugail = shepherd
beibio	a person's name
beili	enclosure (English bailey); or bailiff
beirdd	bards
beistion	beach; seashore; shallows
belan	?round hill
berllan -au	orchard
ben -ni	can mean a waggon; might be a variant of Key Word pen
bencydd	banks; mounds
bendigaid	holy; blessed
ber (1)	short; also fir tree
ber (2) -au -i	roasting spit; spear
bera -u	rick
berem	yeast; a river name
berian	a person's name
beris	a person's name
Berriew	from Welsh: Aber rhiw
Bers	from English: Bersham = river meadows
bert	pretty; fair
berth	hedge(s)
berw or berwr	cress

bery -on	kite
Bethesda	Biblical name, probably first given to a chapel
betws	house of prayer; place of worship
betysau	houses of prayer; places of worship
beudy	cowshed; stall
beulah	a river name; a chapel name (Biblical)
beuno	a saint's name
Bewpyr	from Norman: *Beau pres/repaire*=charming meadow/resting place
bica	pointed
bier	short
big	beak; peak
Bishton	from English: Bishop's town
blaen -a -au -ion	source or upper reaches of a river; the top end of a valley; far uplands
blaidd	wolf
blain -a -au -ion	source or upper reaches of a river; the top end of a valley; far uplands
blas	mansion
bledd	wolf
bleddfach	a person's name
bleddian	a person's name
bledrws	a person's name
bleiddiad	wolves
blodau	flowers
blodyn	flower
bo (1)	dirt; mine
bo (2)	dwelling, from bod
boch -au	cheek; mouth
bod	abode; residence; but a church if followed by a saint's name
boda	buzzard
boeth	warm; hot; burnt
bol (and bola and boly)	hollow; basin; but can, oddly, also mean a hillock
bôn	bottom of; foot of; stump
boncath	buzzard

bont -ydd	bridge; arch over. The name of the river bridged or of a person usually follows
borfa	grazing for cattle
borth	harbour; ferry; gateway
borwen	maid
bot	small house/home; a dwelling (from bod)
brac	malt
bradwen	a person's name
brag	malt
braich -au -iau	promontory; ridge; mountain spur; headland
brain	(black) birds of crow family
braith	speckled; variegated
brân (1)	(black) bird of crow family; also a river name
brân (2)	dark; also a river name
bras	large; rich
bre -oedd -on	highland
brech	mottled; speckled; variegated
Brecknock	from Welsh: Brycheiniog, see **iog**
Brecon	from Welsh: Brycheiniog, see **iog**
brefi	a river name
bren -nau	tree
brengi	a person's name; or Land of Breng
brenhines	queen
brenhinoedd	kings
brenin	king
briallu	primrose
brig -au (1)	top
brigau (2)/brigyn/brig	branches/branch/branch
briog	a saint's name
brith	mottled; speckled; variegated
brithyll -od	trout
briw	?ditch
bro -ydd	region; border; march(es); vale
broch (1)	badger
broch (2)	wild; frothy; foaming
brochwel	a person's name

broga	frog
brogan	meandering; a river name
Brogyntyn	from English: Porkington
Brombil	from English: Broom Hill

bron-au -nydd -oed   slope; breast of hill

bronfraith /bronfreithod	thrush /thrushes
bronwen	weasel
brwnen	rush
brwnt	dirty
brwyn	rushes/a person's name
brwynen	rush
brych	mottled; speckled; variegated
brychan	a person's name
brychein	a person's name
brydan	a river name
brym	hill (from bryn)

bryn -iau -na   bank; mound; mount; hill. A person's name often follows

bryncyn -nau	hillock
buan	a saint's name
buches	cowfold
buchod	cows
buellt	cow pasture, from bu(wch)=cow and (gw)ellt=grass
buga	a river name; perhaps a personal name; maybe a contraction of bugail
bugail	shepherd; also a river name
bugeil -iaid	shepherd
Builth (1)	from Welsh: Buallt (cow pasture, see buellt, just above). Complete Welsh name: Llanfair-ym-Muallt (St Mary's in the pasture)
buwch	cow
bwa	arch
bwch	roebuck
Bwcle	from English: boc=cow and lea=meadow
Bwla	from English: bull; possibly after an old local pub

bwlch   mountain pass; defile

bwll	pit
bwm (y gors)	bittern
bwrdeistref	borough
bwth -yn	hut; cabin; small cottage
bych or bychan	little
bylch -au	mountain pass
byr (1)	a person's name: Pyr
byr (2) -ion	short
bythod	cottages
bythych	a river name
bythynnod	huts; cottages

C

cabal	ferry, from ceubal
caban -au	cabin; den
cad (1) -au -oedd	battle
cad (2)	(as a prefix with streams and rivers) powerful; strong flowing
cadair -au -iau	camp; (seat of); chair
cadarn	strong
cadell	a person's name
cader	camp; (seat of); chair
cadlas	enclosure; camp
cadle	a person's name: Cadell; or, if cad (1) + le, a soldiers' training area
cadles(s)ydd	enclosures
cadnawes	vixen
cadnawon	foxes
cadno	fox
cadnoes	vixen
cadnoid	foxes
cadog	a saint's name: Cadoc
Cadoxton	from English: Cadog's town
cadwal	a person's name
cadwyn -i -au	mountain range

cae -au -oedd   enclosure; field (care here: see key word **caer** just below)

caeo	a person's name
caer -au -oedd	fort; fortified town; stronghold (care here: see Key Word **cae** just above)
Caer-went	from Welsh: Caer + Gwent
Caerdydd	from Welsh: Caer Tyf (Tyf is an early version of Taf (river), hence Cardiff)
Caerleon	from Welsh: Caer llion ar Wysg (Legion's fort on the river Usk)
Caernarfon	from Caer yn arfon
cafell -au	sanctuary
cain	back; ridge; also a river name
caint	a tribal name: Caint
calch	chalk; lime
calchen	limestone
caled	rough; hard
call	a river name
calon	heart
cam (1)	crooked; winding
cam (2) -au	step
camas	river bend
camfa	stile (=cam (2) + fa)
camlas -au -ydd	canal
camlesi	canals
can (1)	white; shining; also form of 100 (number)
cân (2)	song
can (3)	flour
canfed	hundredth (ordinal)
canna	a river name
cannaid	? bright; shining
cannarch	a river name
canol	middle
cant	border; also 100 (number)
canten	a person's name
cantref	a division of land, similar to an English hundred

capel	chapel
caradog	a person's name: Caractacus
Cardiff	English form of Welsh Caerdydd (see above)
Cardigan	English form of Welsh Ceredigion (i.e. Ceredig's land)
caredig	kind; gentle
carlwm or carlwn	stoat
Carmarthen	Welsh: either Caer Fyrddin (Merlin's fort) or, more likely, from caer + *moridunum* (its old Celtic name adapted by the Romans)
carn -au -edd -i -ydd	pile of stones; cairn
carnedd -au	cairn; stones
caron	a person's name
carreg	stone
carrog	stream
cartre(f)/cartrefi	home/homes
carw	red deer stag
caseg	mare
castan	chestnut
castell -au	castle; stronghold; fortified town
cath -od	cat
cathan	a saint's name: Cathen
cathed	a person's name
cathein	a saint's name: Cathen
cathen	a saint's name
catoc	a person's name: Cadoc
catoe	a person's name: Cadoc
catwg	a person's name: Cadoc
cau	sunken; hollow
cawci	jackdaw
cawn -ei	reeds
cawnen	reed
cawr	giant
caws -iau	cheese
cecs	hemlock; also a river name
cedig	a person's name
cedny	foxes

cedwel	a person's name: Cadwal
cedyrn	strong
ceffyl -au	horse

cefn -au -oedd -ydd   mountain ridge; back (of hill)

cefnen	gently rising hill; ridge
cefni	a river name
ceg -au	mouth
cegid	hemlock; also a river name
cegin	jay
cegyr	a river name

cei -au   quay

ceidrych	a person's name
ceiliog -od	cockerel
ceimle	common land
cein	back; ridge
ceinach	hare
ceinwen	a person's name
ceirch	oats
ceiri	giants
ceiriog	a river name; a man's name
ceiro	a person's name
ceirw	red deer stags
celert	a person's name
cell (1)	a person's name
cell (2) -au -oedd	(monk's) cell; chamber

celli -au -oedd   grove; copse

celydd	bower
celyn (1)	holly; also a river name
celyn (2)	a person's name: Celyn; or Cuhelyn
celynnen	holly
cemais	river bend
cen (or cenn) -au	lichen
Cenarth	from Welsh: cen (lichen) + garth (hill; enclosure; ridge)
cendle	a person's name

cenfig	a person's name: Cynffig
cenhinen	leek
cenllif	torrent
cennech	a person's name
cennen	a person's name
cennin	leeks; also a person's name
cer (1)	near
cer (2)	a person's name
ceran	a saint's name
cerdin	a river name
ceredig	a person's name
ceri (1)	a person's name
ceri (2)	Cer + i, i.e. Cer's land
cerist	a river name
cerrig	stones
ceste	a river name
cestyll	castles
cethin	a person's name
ceti	a person's name
ceu (prefix)	hollow
ceubal or ceubol	ferry boat
ceulan	hollow bank of river
ceunant	ravine
cewri	giants; also a river name
ceyrydd	walls; cities; forts; castles
chain	a river name
chwar or chwarel -i -au -ydd quarry	
chwe or chwech	six (number); can also mean sweet, from chweg
chweg	pleasant; sweet
chwerw	bitter
chwil or chwilen/chwilod	beetle/beetles
chwim	fast
chwirl	whirling
chwyn or chwynn	weeds
chwyrn	rapid; swift
chynlleth	a person's name: Cynllaith
cigfran	raven

cil -iau -ie	nook; source of stream; possibly back of

cilen -nau

little corner, or recess

Cilibion	from Welsh: celli + gwlybion (damp groves)
Cimla	from Welsh: ceimle (common lands)
cimla or cimle or cimne or cinme	common land
cimwch	lobster
ciogfran	raven
clai	clay
claif	enclosed place; clay (soil)
clais (1) -iau	stripe
clais (2) -iau	ditch; brook
clas	(monks') cloister
clawdd	dyke; embankment
cledd -au (1)	sword; also a river name
cleddau (2)	a person's name: Gleddyf
cleddy	a river name
cleddyf -au	sword; also a river name
clegr or clergyr	rock(y)
cleiau or cleisiau	clays
cler	a saint's name: Clare
clir	clear
clo	knoll
cloch (1)	bell
cloch (2)	sound; noise
cloddau	dykes; embankments
cloddfa (pl cloddfeydd)	quarry
clog -au	cliff; crag; precipice
clogwyn -i	cliff
cloddiau	dykes; embankments
clos -ydd	yard

clun

moor; meadow. When in the first syllable of a name it can mean vale/glen

clws	pretty; nice
clwyd -au -i	a roost; (used figuratively): a resting place; also a river name
clychau	bells
clydach	a rocky stream
clyn or clyne	meadow; sometimes short for celyn=holly

clynn	a person's name: Gelyn
clynnog	holly-ish: place with lots of holly (from celynnog)
clywedog	a river name
cnau	nuts
cneu -en	nut
cnicht	from English: knight; also a person's name
cob	embankment
coch	red; scarlet
coddiau	banks; ditches (from cloddiau)
codiad	hillocks
coe	wood
coed -an -ydd	forest; wood; trees
coeden	tree
coedwig	forest
coeg	a wood
coel	a person's name
coewig	forest; wood (from coedwig)
cog -au	cuckoo
col	a person's name: Coel
colf	branch
collen	hazel; a saint's name; a river name
colomen	dove
colwyn	a river name
comin or comins	commonland; unenclosed waste land (from English)
commin or commins	commonland; unenclosed waste land (from English)
comwy -ydd	?conifer
cona	a person's name
confoe	a person's name, see cwmboi
Conway	English form of Welsh conwy
conwy	a river name
conysiog	from Welsh: cowys (a name) + iog
copa -au	top; crest
cor (at start of word)	can imply small
corbwyll	whirlpool
cored -au	weir; or a (monks') dam to hold fish
corlan	sheep fold

corn	horn; antler
cornant	brook; small stream
cornel	corner
coron -au	crown
cors -ydd	bog; fen
corsen	reed
Corwen	from Welsh: cor + faen
cothi	a river name
cownwy	a river name
cowys	a name: Conws/?Conwys
cra	a river name
cra or craf	garlic; also a river name
crai	bare; rough; severe. However, if it describes water it can mean fresh; clear
craig	boulder; rock; crag
cras	dry; parched
crawnon	a river name
Cray	English form of Welsh: Crai
crech	rippling
creddyn	easy to defend
cref	strong; also a river name
creigiau	rocks; boulders; crags; cliffs
creu -iau	animal pen; sty
cri	a cry
crib -au	crest; summit; (can also mean thistle)
cribin	a river name
cribyn	crest
Cricieth	from Welsh: Crug + caith (=hill of the bondmen/slaves)
Crickhowell	English form of Welsh: Crug Hywel
crin	dry; withered
crist	Christ

croes cross; crossroad. The cross sign was used to show parish boundaries

croeso hospitality; welcome
crofft croft (from English)
cron round; circular
croyw clear (water etc.)
crug -iau hillock; mound; tump
crwm curved
crwn circular; round
crych rippling; bubbling
cryd back of; ridge
cryf -ion strong; flourishing
crymlyn valley with bend; round shaped valley (from cryn + glyn)

cryn -ion round; circular

crynant from creu + nant; or cryf + nant; another possibility may be crwm + nant = stream with a bend in it

crynion round
cryw weir
crywyn fold; pen
cuan owl
cul -ion narrow
culfor -oedd strait; sea channel
cun lovely
cunnah a person's name
curig a person's name
cwar -rau quarry
cwch boat
cwcod cuckoos
cwcw cuckoo

cwm (1) a bowl shaped valley or depression in land; a vale; a glen

cwm (2) (found less often) a shortened form of cwmwd or cymwyd; that is, either a commot, a community smaller than an (English) hundred, or an old measure of land

cwmboi	a river name, possibly a corruption of personal name, Confoe/Convoi
cwmin	commonland; unenclosed wasteland (from English)
cwna	a person's name
cwningen/cwningod	rabbit/rabbits
cwr	corner; border
Cwrlwys	from English: Culverhouse (dovecote)
cwrt	court; mansion
cwt (1)	tail; tail-like; can also (when used with streams) mean short
cwt (2)	hut
cwtiau	tails; like tails
cybi	a person's name
cychod	boats
cydweli	Cadwal's lands or Cedwel's lands
cyfail	a person's name: Cyfeiliog
cyfarthen	battle
cyfeiliog	a person's name
cyffin -iau -ydd	(joint) boundary; in plural, means adjoining lands
cyfodiad	hillock
cyll	hazel trees
cymer -au	confluence; a place where streams and/or rivers meet
cymoedd	vales; valleys
Cymru	Wales
cyn	early
cynan	a person's name
cynfall	a saint's name
cynfelin	a person's name: Cymbeline
cynffig	a person's name
cynidr	a person's name
cynlais	a person's name
cynllaith	a person's name; also a river name
cynnes	warm
cynog	a person's name
cynon	a person's name; also a river name
cynraidd	a person's name

cynt(af)	first
cynwrig	a person's name
cynwyd	a person's name
cynwyl	a saint's name
cyrn	antlers; horns
cyrtiau	court; mansion
cytau	tails; like tails
cyter or cytir -oedd	common land
cytiau (1)	tails; like tails
cytiau (2)	huts; pens; sties
cywair	a person's name
cywarch	flax; a river name
cywyn	a river name

D

da	livestock; goods
daear	earth
daethwy	(see Aethwy)
daf	large: a river name (from taf)
dafad	sheep
dafn	drop
dafydd	a person's name: David
dai (1)	houses
dai (2)	a person's name: Davy
dail	leaves

dan   below; under

danadl	nettles
dand	nettle
danglwys	a person's name: Tanglwys
danheddog	jagged
dâr	oak trees; a river name
darcy	a person's name: D'Arcy
dare	a river name, an anglicized form of dar
darn -au	part, piece of land
daron	a river name
darren	rocky hillside
dau	two
dawe	a river name
ddaear	earth

52

ddafad	sheep
ddâr	oaks
dde or de	south; southern
ddeg	ten
ddein(i)ol	biblical name: Daniel
dderw	oaks; a river name
ddinas -oedd	fort; later, a city
ddion	black (plural form)
ddofn	deep
ddoged	a person's name: Doged

ddôl -au riverside meadow

ddraig	dragon
ddu -on	black
ddŵr	water
ddwy	two
ddyn	fortification; height
de (1)	south; southern
de (2)	when de (a form of tŷ/dŷ) comes after the word llan and immediately before a saint's name, it signifies a high level of (religious) respect, implying something like 'the most holy', perhaps
deau	south; southern
dee	a river name
defaid	sheep (plural)
defnyn	drop
deg (1)	ten

deg (2) fair; beautiful

degan	a person's name: Tegan
degann	a tribal name (Latin *Decantae*)
degar	a person's name: Tegyr
degfan	a person's name: Tegfan
degfedd	a saint's name: Tegfedd
degla	a person's name: Tegla
degyr	a person's name: Tegyr
deildy	bower
deilen	leaf

deilo	a saint's name: Teilo
deiniol	a saint's name: Daniel
deio	a person's name: Davy
deiri	oaks
del	hard; harsh; (but after about 1900, pretty; neat)
delerch	a person's name
delyn	harp
Denbigh	from Welsh: din + bychan (small fort)
denni	a person's name: Tenni
dennis	English form of dinas
denoi	a saint's name: Tenoi; or de + Noe (another saint)
deri	oak trees: also a river name
derlwyn	oak grove

derw -en oak tree; also a river name

derwydd	druid; otherwise derw + gwŷdd (i.e. oakwood)
deryn	bird(s)
deu	two
deulwyddog	a saint's name: Teulwyddog
dewi	a saint's name: David
dibyn	precipice
diffaeth	wilderness
diffwys -au -ydd	steep slope
dilyw	flood

din fort; city

dinam or dinan	fortified
dinas -oedd	large town; fortress; refuge
Dinbych	from din and bychan, i.e. small fort
dingad	a saint's name
diolwg	ugly
dir	land
disglair	bright
dlos	pretty; beautiful
dochau	a person's name
doged	a person's name

54

dôl -au -e -ydd riverside meadow

dolan meandering
dolenn meandering
domen mound; motte
don (1) wave

don (2) lay land, not natural meadow but previously tilled land given over to grass

donat a saint's name
dorthy a person's name
dou two
dough a person's name: Dochau
Dovey from Welsh: dyfi (dark); a river name
doylan from Welsh: deu +lwyn
draen or draenen thorn
draenog hedgehog
draeth beach
draig dragon
drain thorns
dre or dref home
drin -oedd battle
drobwll whirlpool
droed (at) foot of
Drope Swedish viking: *thorpe* (village)
dros across; over
drud -ion rugged; harsh
drudwy starling

drum -au -iaf -io crest of mountain; ridge

drws pass; gap through mountain
drys -i brambles; tangled
drysau/drysiau passes; gaps through mountains
dryslwyn brambly thicket
dryw wren
du -on black; dark
duar a river name
dudno a person's name: Tudno
dulais a river name

Dunvant	from Welsh: Dwfn + nant
dutglyd	a person's name: Tutglyd
dwf	deep; dense; also a river name
dwfn	deep; dense; also a river name
dwfr	water (in all its senses)
dŵr (1)	water (in all its senses)
dŵr (2)	tower
dwrgi	otter
dwrn	a person's name
dwy	two; also a river name
dwym	warm
dwyrain	east
dwywe	a person's name
dŷ (1) or dy (1)	house
dŷ (2) or dy (2)	when dŷ or dy (both are a form of tŷ) comes after the word llan and immediately before a saint's name, it signifies a high level of (religious) respect implying something like 'most holy', perhaps
dybie	a saint's name: Tybiau or Tybie
dyfan	a person's name
dyfed (1)	?deep
Dyfed (2)	pre-Roman lands of *Demetae* tribe
dyffrin -oedd -noedd	vale, bottom; valley
dyffryn -oedd	vale, bottom; valley
dyfi	a river name
dyfn	deep; dense
dyfnant	a river name
dyfnion	deep
dyfodwg	a saint's name: Tyfodwg
dyfr -au	water (in all its senses)
dyfrdwy	a river name
dyfredd	waters (in all senses)
dyfrig	a saint's name
dyfroedd	waters (in all senses)
dyn	fortification; height
Dynfant	corruption of Welsh: Dwfn + nant
dyrys	thorny; tangled undergrowth

dysgynni	a river name
dysilio	a man's name: Tysilio
dysul	a person's name: Tysul
dywyl	dark; gloomy
dywyll	dark

E

eang	wide; extensive
eb	colt(s) or horse(s), from ebol(ion)
ebbw	from an earlier river name (Ebwydd from ?eb + gwyllt: ? wild horses)
ebol -ion	colt; horse
ebwy	see ebbw, just above
eccle	from an English word meaning a church
ecleis/ecles	from an English word meaning a church
edeirn	a person's name: Edern
edelig	a person's name
eden	a river name
edern	a person's name: Eternus
ederyn	birds
edw	a river name
edych	a person's name
efail	smithy; forge
efenechtyd	monastery
efrog	a person's name; or efwr + og (suggesting an abundance of cow parsnip)
efwr	cow parsnip
efyrnwy	a river name
eglir	clear
eglwys -i	church
egri	a person's name
egwad	a person's name
ehedydd	skylark
eiddew	ivy; also a person's name
eidion -nau	bullocks
eifl	opinions differ: ?gap between two peaks or ?two tines
eilfed	second (ordinal)
einion	a person's name
einon	a person's name; also a river name
eira	snow

eirian	bright; beautiful
eirlys	snowdrop; also a person's name
eirth	bears; also a river name
eithaf	remote; furthest
eithew	ivy
eithin -yn	gorse; furze
eithon	a person's name
elai	a river name
elan	a person's name; also a river name
elen	a person's name
elerch	a person's name
eleri	a person's name
elidir	a person's name; also a river name
elli	a person's name; also a river name
elwyddan	a person's name
elyf	cattle
elyrch	swans
elystan	a person's name
emlyn	a person's name
emrys	a person's name: Ambrose
en (at end of words)	suggests little or small
enfys -au	rainbow
engyll	a river name
eog	salmon
eos	nightingale
epynt	horses' trail; tracks: from eb + hynt
erch	frightful; also speckled; also a river name
erdd	old word for high land
erddig	from an English name: Eurdic
ermid	hermit
erth	bears
erw -au	Celtic measure of land (varying in size with degree of difficulty of farming it); an estate
erwyd	a person's name
eryr -i -od (1)	rising ground
eryr -od -on (2)	eagle
eryri	highlands, from eryr (1); or the land of the eagle, from eryr (2). This is also the Welsh name for the English Snowdonia
esgair	mountain spur; ridge
esgeib	bishop

esgob -ion	bishop
esgor	elder
esgyll	wings
Estyn	from English: East town
eugrad	a person's name
euraid	golden
eurig	a person's name: Meurig
ewenny	a person's name
ewig	doe; hind
ewryd	a person's name
eynon	a person's name

F

fa (at end of words)	spot; place
fach (1)	small
fach (2)	a nook; a bend in a river
fadog	a person's name: Madoc
faelog	a saint's name: Maelog
faen (1)	vein of mineral ore, or of stone
faen (2)	stone
faen (3)	an old tribal name
faenol	manor; court
faenor	manor or chief's home
faer (1)	bailiff or steward: see maer for more detail
faer (2)	mayor
faerdre	a bonded village under the authority of a steward
faes	meadow
faglan	personal name: Baglan
fagu	a person's name
fagwyr	walls; rocky place
fai	field; plain; level terrain
fair	the Madonna's name; Mary
fâl	dale; vale
faldwyn	a person's name: Maldwin, Baldwin
fan (1)	peak
fan (2) (at end of word)	spot; place
fasi	an English name: Massy
fathew	a river name

fawn	peat
fe	plain
fecca	a person's name: Becca
fech (with/in river names)	small
fechan	small; also a river name
fedwen	birch tree; a river name
feini	veins of mineral ores, or of stone
feirion	a person's name: Meirion
felan	yellow or brown
felanog	cowslip
felen	brown or yellow
felin -au	mill
fellte	a person's name: Mellte
felyn	yellow; golden
fendigaid	holy
fer	short; also fir tree
fera	hay rick
ferin	a person's name: Merin
fern	a person's name
Ferwig	from English: Berwic (=barley farm)
feurig	a person's name: Meurig
feydd	can be plural of word-ending fa
feyr	a person's name: Mair, Mary
ffair	fair; market
ffald (or ffalt) -au -e	fold; pen; farmyard
ffawydd/en	beeches/beech

fferm -ydd   farm

ffestin	a person's name
ffili	a person's name
ffin -iau	boundary; limit
Fflint	from English: flint; hard rock
ffordd	road; route
Ffordun	English ford + tun: farm near river crossing
fforest -ydd	forest; open country; parkland
ffos	ditch; dyke; moat
ffraid	a saint's name: Bridget, Bride
ffranc	(Norman) French
ffrau	a river name
ffraw	swift stream

ffridd   rough mountain pasture; moorland; sheep walk

   ffrwd   swift stream; torrent
   ffrwyn -au   bridle
   ffrydiau   swift flowing streams; torrents
   ffwlbart   polecat
   ffwrn   oven
   ffwyst   a saint's name
   ffynhonnau   fountains
   ffynnog   a person's name

ffynnon -au   source; spring; well; fountain

   ffyr   fir tree
   ffyrdd   roads; routes
   ffyrniau   ovens
   ficer -iaid   vicar
   fign or figyn   bog; marsh
   fihangel   a saint's name: Mihangel, Michael
   filltir   mile
   foch   cheek
   foel (1) -ydd   hill
   foel (2) -ion   bare
   foist   a saint's name: Ffwyst
   for (at end of a word)   implies large
   forus   a person's name: Morris
   forwyn   maid
   fraid   a saint's name: Bridget, Bride
   frain   (black) birds of crow family
   fraith   speckled
   frân   (black) bird of crow family
   fre   hill
   frenhines   queen
   frenin   king
   friog   a saint's name: Briog
   fro -ydd   region
   frogan   meandering; a river name
   fron -ydd   hillside
   front   dirty
   fryda   a person's name
   fuan   a saint's name: Buan

fuches	pasture for cows
fudr	polluted
fwrog	a person's name: Mwrog
fychan (1)	a person's name: Vaughan
fychan (2)	small
fynwy	a river name
fynydd	mountain
fyr	short; also fir tree
fyrddin	a person's name: Morddyn = Merlin

G

gabal	ferry boat
gad -au	battle
gadair	camp; (seat of)
gader	camp; fort
gadfan	a person's name: Cadfan
gadog	a person's name: Cadog
gaeaf -au	winter
gaeo	a person's name
gaer -au	fort; camp
gafr	goat
gaint	a tribal name: Caint
gair	a river name
galed	rough; hard
gallt	wooded hillside
gam	crooked, winding
gamfa	stile
ganol	middle
ganten	a person's name: Canten
gapel	chapel
gar (1)	rough
gar (2)	near
gardd	garden; enclosure
garedig	kind
garlleg	garlic
garmon	a saint's name
garn -au	cairn; stones
garnedd -au	cairn; stones
garon	a person's name: Caron
garrog	stream; brook

garth (1)	hill; enclosure; mountain ridge; uncultivated land
garth (2)	a person's name
garw -on	rugged; craggy; rough
gaseg	mare
gastell -au	castle; stronghold; fortified town
gasteyn	a person's name
gasty	a person's name: Gasteyn
gât -iau	gate
gathan	a saint's name: Cathen
gatwg	a person's name: Cadog
gau	closed
gavenny	from Welsh: gofenny (?iron smith)
gefail	forge; smithy
gefenni	a river name
geg -au	mouth
geifr	goats
geillt	wooded hillsides
geirwon	rugged; craggy; rough
gelau or gelen	leech; also a river name
gele	a river name
gelert	a person's name: Celert
gell -au -ioedd (1)	(monk's) cell; chamber
gelli -au -oedd (2)	(small) wood grove
gelltydd	wooded hillsides
gelod	leeches
gelyn	a person's name
gelynen	a river name
gelynnen	holly tree
genau	entrance to valley; estuary
gennech	a person's name: Cennech
gennith	a person's name: Cynnydd
ger	near
geraint	a person's name: Gerontius
gerddi	gardens
geti	a person's name: Ceti
gigfran	raven
gil	recess; nook
glais	stream; brook; ditch

glân (2)	beautiful; clean; holy
glas	a colour that can be anywhere between green and blue
glaslyn	a river name
glaswellt(yn)	grass
gledd -au	sword; a river name
gleis -ion	a colour that can be anywhere between green and blue
glennydd	river banks; sea shores
glesyn	borage
glo	coal; charcoal; shining
gloddfa -gloddfeydd (pl)	quarry
gloew	shining
glog -au	knoll; rock
gloyw -on	bright; shiny
gludair	heap of stones
glyn -noedd	vale
glyn dŵr	a person's name: Glendower
glywis	a person's name
Gnoll	English: knoll
go (1)	quite; rather
go (2)	under; near; can also mean blacksmith (from gof)
goch	red; scarlet
godre -on	border; edge; bottom
goe	wood
goed	wood
goedwig	forest
goedydd	woods
goeg	wood
goetre	farm near wood
gof -aint	blacksmith; iron smith
gofer	small stream; brook
gog -au	cuckoo
gogledd	north; northern
gogo(f)	cave; lair; an old parish name (in Cardigan)
golau	light
golch	a wash
gollen	a saint's name: Collen

golosg	charcoal
golwg	sight
golyg -on	sight; a look
gorlan	fold
gorlech	a river name
gorllewin	west
gors	bog; fen
gorsaf	station
gorwel -ion	horizon
gorwydd	edge of forest
gothi	a river name: Cothi
gownwy	a river name
goy	wood
graig -iau	rock; crag
grech	rippling
gref	strong
greigiau	boulders; rocks; crags
griafol	mountain ash tree
gribin	crest
gris -iau	step
grist	Christ
gro	pebbles; pebbly
groes	cross; crossroad
grom	curved
gron	round; circular
gros	cross; cross-road
groyw	fresh; clear
gruffudd	a person's name: Griffith
gruffydd	a person's name: Griffith
grug (1) -oedd	heath; heather
grug (2) -iau	hillock; tump
grwn	ridge
grwyne	a river name
Grysmwnt	from Norman French: *Gros mont*=large hill
guernol	swallow
gul	narrow
gunfall	a saint's name: Cynfall
gurig	a person's name: Curig
gwaelod -ion	low region; low ground
gwag	empty
gwair	hay; grass

gwaith	a (coal) mine
gwal -au -iau	wall
gwâl	lair
gwalch	hawk
gwas	servant
gwastad	flat land
gwaun	high and wet level land moor; meadow; also a river name
gwawr	dawn
gwcw	cuckoo
gwden	a river name
gweigion	empty
gweir	grass; hay
gweision	servants
gwell	better; superior
gwellt	sward
gwelltyn	grass
gwely	bed; resting place for animals
gwen	fair (adjective)
gwenarth	a person's name
gwendraeth	a river name
gwenith	wheat
gwenlais	a river name
gwenllian	a person's name
gwennol	swallow
gwent	field; plain; market venue
gwenyn/gwenynen	bees/bee
gwerful	a person's name
gwern -ydd	marsh; can also mean alder trees
gwernen	alder
gwersyllt	from an old English name for a hangman's hill
gwested	flat land
gwesty	stall (animals); inn
gwesym	a river name
gwesyn	a river name
gweunon	high and level wetlands
gweunydd	moors; meadows; high and wet level land
gweynen	bee
gwiail	rods; switches

gwialen	rod; twig
gwiber	viper
gwig (1) -au -oedd	cove; open, unsheltered bay (Viking: *vik*)
gwig (2) -au -oedd	wood; grove; also hamlet
gwili	a river name
gwilym	a person's name: William
gwiwer -od	red squirrel
gwlad	district; realm; open country
gwladus	a person's name
gwledig	lord; ruler
gwledydd	districts; realms; open country
gwlith -oedd	dew
gwlyb -ion	wet (lands)
gwr (1)	corner; edge
gŵr (2)	man
gwrach -od -iod -en	witch; also a river name
gwran	little man
gwrda(f)	a person's name
gwrtheyrnion	a person's name
gwrych -oedd	hedge
gwy or gwyon	water; the Welsh name for the river Wye
gŵydd (1)	goose
gŵydd (2)	wild; fallow; uncultivated; desolate. Can also mean a tomb
gwŷdd (3)	trees; forest
gwyddel(an)	a person's name
gwydderig	a river name
gwyddfarch	a person's name
gwyddfid	honeysuckle
gwydir	low lying land
gwydr -au	glass
gwydyr	?gwy + tir
gwyla or gwylan -od	seagull
gwyllt -ion	wild
gwymon	seaweed
gwyn -ion	white; light; shining; brilliant
Gwynedd	northern Wales (lands of *Venedotae* tribe)
gwynfai	river
gwynfi	a person's name
gwynne	white; shining
gwynt -oedd	wind

gwynwarwy	a saint's name
gŵyr (1)	crooked
gŵyr (2)	English: Gower; meaning is uncertain
gwyrdd	green
gwyros	privet
gwyw	withered
gybi	a person's name: Cybi
gyfail	a person's name: Cyfeiliog
gyffin	edge; limit
gyll	hazel trees
gymer -au	place where streams and/or rivers meet
Gymru	Wales
gynfall	a person's name: Cynfall
gynfelin	a person's name: Cynfelin, Cymbeline
gynidr	a person's name: Cynidr
gynlais	a person's name: Cynlais
gynnydd	a person's name: Cynnydd
gynolwen/gynolwyn	a person's name; also a river name
gyr -roedd	drove
gyrn	cairns
gywraidd	a person's name: Cynraidd

H

hadau	seeds
haearn	iron
hafan	haven; anchorage
hafn	gorge; ravine
hafod -au -ydd	upland summer farmstead (compare hendre(f))
hafon	haven
hafren	a river name: the English river Severn
halen	salt; brine
halwyn	salt
Hanmer	from English: Han's (i.e. Hagena's) + mer (lake)
haran	a person's name
harbwr	harbour
hardd	beautiful
Harlech	from hardd + llech (beautiful rock)
Harn	from Welsh: Treharn

haul	sun
Hawarden	from English: High Worthing
hawdd	pleasant; easy
hawys	a person's name
hebog -au	peregrine falcon; (generic) hawk
hedydd	skylark
hedyn	seed
heilwen	sunshine (= heulwen)
heilyn	a person's name
hêl	flat riverside land
helfa/helfydd (pl)	hunting ground
heli or hell	salt water; sea
helyg	willow trees
helygen	willow
hen	old (but see hendre, too)
hendre or **hendref**	winter dwelling in a valley, to which people and their animals returned after spending summer in their hafod
hendrefydd	winter dwellings in a valley, to which people and their animals returned after spending summer in their hafod
heol -ydd	road
hesb	dry; barren
hesg	sedges
hesp	dry; barren
heulwen	sunshine
hewl -ydd	road
heylin	a person's name
hilari	a saint's name
hillet	a person's name: Hiledd
hir -ion	long
hiraeth	a river name
hirin	a river name
hirwaun	from hir + (g)waun; also a river name
hirwern	a river name
hodd/hoddni	a river name
hodni	a river name (= hoddni)
hoff	pleasant; easy

hoffa	a person's name
holl	whole
honddu	a river name
hopcyn	a person's name: Hopkin
howey	from Welsh: Hywi; also a river name
howni	a river name
hudol	enchanting
hwfa	a person's name
hwnt	over there
hwrdd	ram
hyddgen	a person's name
hydfer	a river name
hydref	autumn
hyfryd	pleasant; easy
hyll	ugly
hynt -iau -oedd	way; course; track
hysb	dry; barren
hywi	a river name

I

iaeth	a river name
iago	a person's name: James
ianto	a person's name: Evan
iar	hen; fowl
iarll	earl
iddon	a person's name
idris	a person's name
ieirll	earls
iet -au	gate
ifan	a person's name, Evan, Ivan
ilan	a person's name; also a river name
illog	a person's name
illterne	a person's name: Illteyrn
illtud	a saint's name
Ilston	English version of Welsh: Llanilltud Gŵyr
in (at the end of a name)	originally meant people of or descendants of (the named person), so Glywysing meant (King) Glywis's people, or his lands
ing (at the end of a name)	originally meant people of or descendants of the (named person) as **in** just above

ioan	a person's name: John
iog (1) (at the end of a word)	means -y, or -ish, as hilly, or steepish
iog (2) (after a name)	means possessions of or lands of (the named person), so Brycheiniog or Brechiniog meant (King) Brychan's lands
iolo	a person's name
iolyn	a person's name
ion (after a name)	means possessions of (the named person); see **iog (2)** above
Ion, or Ior	the Lord
ior (at the end of a word)	can suggest a lot of (what that word means)
iorwerth	a person's name
iorwg	ivy
irfon	a river name
is (1)	court, from llys
is (2)	can mean: this side, or our side (compare ar); or below
isaf	lowest
isha	lowest
ishen	a person's name: Isien
issac	a person's name: Isaac
ithel	a person's name
ithfaen	granite
ithon	a river name
iwan	a person's name: Evan
iwrch	roebuck (stag)

J

There is no **J** in the Welsh alphabet, though there are a few non-Welsh words starting with **J**.

K

There is no **K** in the Welsh alphabet, but there are some anglicized names, such as :

Kenfig	English version of person's name: Cynffig
Kerry	English version of person's name: Ceri
Kidwelly	English version of Welsh: Cedwel + i = Cedwel's land, or Cadwel's land

la or lais	stream; brook
lafar	babbling; loud
Lampeter	English version of the Welsh: Llanbedr Pont Steffan
Lamphey	a corruption of the Welsh: Llandyfái
lan (1)	up hill; slope
lan (2) -nau -noedd	(parish) church, see **llan**
lan (3)	bank (of river or stream), from glan
lann	corruption of llan
las	a colour anywhere between blue and green
Laugharne	Welsh: Talacharn
lawn	full
lawnyd	a person's name
le	place
lefrith	in place-names probably a variant of lle + ffridd; also means milk
leg	slate
leon	(Roman) legion
leri	a person's name: Eleri
leucu	a saint's name: Lucy
Libanus	Biblical name: Lebanon
libart	land around/surrounding a dwelling
lili	lily
lin	flax; also a river name
linog	fox, possibly from llwyn and og
lion	(Roman) legion, lleng in Welsh
Lisvane	from Welsh: Llys + faen
llaca	mud
lladd	slaughter
llaeth	milk
llaid	mud
llain	strip of land
llaith (1)	damp
llaith (2)	death

llan (1) -nau — church (of); also parish (of). Llan is nearly always followed by a saint's name. There are so many saints' names, both male and female, which appear in Welsh place-names – coming from the fifth to the tenth centuries in particular – that they could never all be included in a list such as this one. Indeed, given the number of localized spellings, especially of originally Latin or Latinized saints' names, even the collection of all the names would be a considerable undertaking. Originally, llan just meant a farm dwelling or place set aside for a special purpose

llan (2) (much rarer)	llan preceding a river name is sometimes a corrruption of glan/glannau
Llanboidy	a corruption of nant+ beudy
Llandarcy	mixed: Welsh (llan) and English (D'Arcy, a family name)
Llandovery	Welsh: Llanymddyfri
llanerch or llannerch	glade; or clearing
Llantony	English version from Welsh: Llanddewi Nant Hodni
Llantwit	English version from Welsh: Llanilltud
llawen	joyful
llawn	full
llawr	bottom; low ground
lle -oedd	place; place of
llech -au -i	slate; a flat stone (and by association, gravestone); rock
llechen	a slate
llechi	slates
llechryd	a river name
llechwedd -au -i	slope
llecyn	a spot
lledr	a river name
llefenny	a river name
lleian -od	nun
lleiniau	strips of land
lleng -oedd	Roman legion
llenydd	(parish) churches
lleon	(Roman) legion
llethr -au	slope; sharp descent
llety -au	lodging; smallholding
lleucu	a saint's name: Lucy
llew -od	lion

Lleweni	Llawen's land
lleyn (1)	a long narrow strip of land
Lleyn (2)	ancient land of the *Lageni* tribe
llia	a river name
llibio	a person's name
llidiard -au	gateway; canal lock; harbour
llidiart	gate
llin	flax; also a river name
llinos -od	linnet
llion	(Roman) legion
lliw -iau	colour; also a river name
lloches -au	refuge; place of safety
llon (at the end of a word)	like the English -ful, as in wonderful, powerful etc.
llong -au	ship
llosg	burnt
lluest -au	hut; temporary abode; small farm
llugan	a river name
llugwy	a river name
llus	whinberries
llwch (1)	pool; bog; swampy
llwch (2)	fishponds or lakes used by monks for catching/storing fish
llwchwr (1)	wet places; marshes
llwchwr (2)	Welsh version of Latin river name: *leuca*
llwm	barren; bare
llwybr -au	path; track
llwyd	grey; also a person's name: Lloyd
llwyf/llwyfen	elms/elm

llwyn -au -i -ydd   a grove; a bush

llwynog -od	fox
llychau	pools; bogs
llydan or llydain	wide
llyfn -ion	smooth
llyfnant	a river name

llyn (1) -au -iau -oedd   lake; large pool

Llŷn (2)   older spelling of Lleyn (2)

llynaid	barren; bare
llynfi	a river name
llynnaid	bare
llynteg	a river name
llys -oedd	court; palace
llysiau	herbs
llywyr	?refuge; place of safety
login	a person's name; or possibly from halogyn: a polluted stream
lon (1) (at the end of a word)	the English -ful, as in wonderful etc.
lôn (2) -ydd	lane
Loughor	English version of Welsh: (Cas)llwchwr (2)
Ludlow	English version of Welsh: Llwydlo
lwch	swampy
lwyn	bush; thicket
lydan	wide; broad
lyn	lake

M

ma (1)	place; spot
ma (2)	very old name for plain; meadow
mablau	burial place
mabli	a person's name
machno	a person's name; also a river name
machreth	a person's name
Machynlleth	plain of Cynllaith (a person's name)
madoc	a person's name: Maddocks
madog	a person's name: Madoc
mael (1) -ion	a prince; a person's name
mael (2) -ydd	hill (from moel)
maelfa -oedd -on	market place
maelgwn or maelgyn	a person's name: Maelgwn
maelien	a person's name
maelog	a saint's name
maen	stone; especially when the stone has a special significance or purpose
maenyn	lump of stone
maenol or maenor	manor; lordship; estate; also a former Welsh territorial/administrative unit containing various townships

maer (1)	steward or reeve: the administrative officer/agent of Welsh court of law
maer (2)	mayor
maes	field; open, not wooded, country
Maesaleg	from Welsh: Bassaleg, from Maes Aleg, or Latin: *basilica*=church
mafon/mafren	raspberries
magon	berries
Magor	from Welsh: Magwyr
magwy	a river name, from magwyr
magwyr -au -i -od -ydd	stone; wall; fortification
mai	plain; level terrain
main (1)	rock
main (2)	thin; narrow
mair	the Madonna's name; Mary
mais	field; open, not wooded, country
maldwyn	a person's name: Baldwin
Malpas	from Norman Latin: *mal*=difficult + *pas*=pass
man -nau	place; spot; also plain
manor	manor (also an old land division)
mans	manse
march (1) (care with marchnad)	horse
march (2)	as an adjective applied to plant names, means big and strong
marchell	a person's name
marchnad	market; forum
marchog -au -oedd -on	knight; rider
Marcross	from Welsh: march (1) + rhos
mari	a person's name: Mari or Mary
marian	moraine; strand
marl	marl (soil)
mars -oedd	marches; borderlands
masarn/masarnen	sycamore, or maple
mawdd	a person's name
mawddach	a river name
mawn -en	peat
meddrod -au	grave; tomb
medrod -au	grave; tomb

meddyg -on	doctor
mefen	a person's name
mefus	wild strawberry
meidr	narrow lane
meidwy -aid -od	recluse; hermit
meillion/meillionen	clovers/clover
mein	narrow
meini	stones; rocks
meinin	(of) stone
meirch	horses
meirion	a person's name
meirl	good earth(s)
meis	field
mêl	honey
melan	yellow or brown
melangell	a person's name
melanog	cowslip
melin -au	mill
mellte	a person's name; a river name
Melltun	from the English name: Mellington
meloch	a river name
melus	sweet
melyn	brown or yellow
melys	sweet
men (1) -nau	spot; position; also a plain
men (2) -ni	waggon
menai	a river name; a person's name derived from the river name
menechi	monks' land
menfor	straits; channel; from main (2) and môr
menig	(fox)glove
menyn	butter
Mera	from English: meer or mere
Merioneth	from Welsh: Meirion + ydd (lands of Meirion)
merlod	ponies
merlyn	pony
mers -ydd	borderlands; lowlands
merthyr -on	martyr's or saint's grave; sanctified cemetery
mesen	acorn
mesydd	fields
meudwy -aid -od	hermit

meurig	a person's name: Maurice
miaren or mieren	briar
mieri	blackberry bushes
mign (or mignen) -au -edd -ioedd	quagmire; bog
mihangel	a saint's name: Michael
miheli	a river name
miheryn	a river name
mill	viola
milltir -oedd	an old Welsh distance unit of about four miles; nowadays just one mile
min -(i)au -ion -oedd	edge; brink; limit; margin
miwl	a river name
moch/mochyn	pigs/pig
mocyn	a person's name: Morgan
modlen	a saint's name: Magdalene
moel (1) -iaid -ion	bare; barren; bald
moel (2) -ydd	(bare) mountain; treeless hill
mold (1)	a person's name
Mold (2)	from Norman French: *Mont hault*=high hill
Monmouth	Welsh: Mynwy (river)
monnow	a river name: from Mynwy
môr -oedd	sea; ocean
morben	headland
morddin	a person's name: Merlin
morfa -u	sea marsh; fen
morfan -nau	sea shore
morfur -(i)au -(i)oedd	sea wall
Morgannwg	Morgan's land (English: Glamorganshire)
mortyn	a person's name: Morton
morus	a person's name: Morris
moryd -iau	estuary
morys	a person's name: Morris
Mostyn	from the English: Mos=swamp+ tun= enclosure; dwelling
Mumbles	from Norman French: *Mammelles*=breasts (two rocks offshore)
mur -(i)au) -(i)oedd	wall; fortification
mwd	mud
mwn -au	mineral ores
mwnt -au	mound

mwt	mud
mwyaf	chief; major
mwyalch or mwyalchen	blackbird
mwyar/mwyaren	blackberries/blackberry
mwyn (1) -(i)on	mild; gentle; pleasant; fair
mwyn (2) -au -i -ydd	mineral; ore; mine
mwyn (3)	treasure; wealth
myn	spot; position
mynach	monk; also a river name
mynachlog -ydd	monastery
mynahod	monasteries
mynaich	monks
mynau	mineral ores; mines
mynech	monk; also a river name
mynis	a person's name
mynod	monks
mynwent -au -ydd	burial ground

mynydd -oedd   mountain

myrddin   a person's name: Merlin

N

nadredd	snakes
nafon	a person's name
nan (1)	brook; stream; sometimes the deep valley or gorge cut by the brook
nan (2)	a person's name
nannau	brooks; streams

nant -au   brook; stream; sometimes the deep valley or gorge cut by the brook

Narberth	from Welsh: yn Arberth
narfon	from Welsh: yn + arfon
naw	nine
Neath	from Latin river name: *Nidum* (Welsh for Neath is Castell Nedd)
nefyn	a person's name
neidr	snake
nen	ridge; summit

nennig or nentig	small stream
nentydd	brooks; streams
neuadd -au	hall; mansion; house of nobleman
Nevern	from Welsh: Nyfer or Nant nyfer
Nevin	English version of Welsh: Nefin
newydd -ion	new
ninian	a saint's name
Nishton	from the Welsh: yn Iston, or Ynys ton
Niwbwrch	from the English: New Borough
niwl -oedd	fog
noddiant	refuge
noddfa/noddfeydd	refuge/refuges
noeth -ion	bare; exposed; bleak
noi	a saint's name: Noe
non/nonna	a saint's name
nos -au	night
nynia	a saint's name
nynio	a person's name: Nynnid
nynnid	a person's name
nyth	nest

O

o	of; out of
ochr -au	side; hillside
odfa	hide-out
odo	a person's name
odwyn	a person's name
odyn	a person's name
odyn -au	lime kiln
oedfa	hide-out
oen	lamb
oer	cold
oeth	a tribal name
og (at the end of a word)	like the English -ish, or -ey, or -y, as in pinkish, milky, etc.
ogfaenen/ogfaen	hawthorn/hawthorn bushes
ogmore	a person's name: Ocmur
ogo	cave; den; lair
ogof -au -eydd	cave; den; lair
Olchfa	from Welsh: Golch + fa, place for washing animals (before market)

ongl -au	corner; angle
onn/onnen	ash trees/ash tree
or (at the end of a word)	can suggest a lot of; e.g. mawnor, a lot of peat
orchy	a person's name: Orchwy
orci	a person's name: Orchwy
oriel -au	gallery; also a river name
orsaf	station
orweg	a person's name: Orwic
orwic	a person's name
orwid	a person's name
orwig	a person's name: Orwic
os (at the end of a plant or tree name)	suggests abundance e.g. Bedwas, from Bedw and os
ostle -au -oedd	inn
ostri -au	lodging; inn
oswald	a person's name
oswallt	a person's name: Oswald
Oswestry	from English: Oswald's tree
owain	a person's name: Owen
owen	a person's name
oyre	cold; or, in south Wales, gold (a mis-spelling in either case)

P

pabell	pavilion; tent
pabo	a saint's name
padarn	a saint's name
padfan	a person's name
padrig	a saint's name: Patrick
paen	a person's name: Payne
pân (1)	fulled cloth, i.e. wool washed and thickened by a fuller
pan (2)	cotton grass
pannau	hollows
pant -au -iau	(shallow) valley or hollow
parc -iau	parkland
parl -au	parley; talk
pawl	a person's name: Paul
pebid	a person's name

peblig	a person's name
pebyll	shelter; cottage; also tents
pedair	four
pedr	a saint's name: Peter
pedwar	four
peithnant	a river name
pellaf	farthest
Pembroke	English from Welsh: Pen + fro

pen -nau   chief; main; head; top; end

penarth	promontory
Pendine	from Welsh: either Pen + tywyn (main beach; top of shore), or Pen + din
penlas (penleision pl.)	cornflower
pennar	name of stream, possibly from penardd
Pennard or Penardd or Penarth	from Welsh: pen + ardd or pen + arth; promontory; cape; ridge of land
penrhyn -nau -noedd	cape; promontory
pentai	huts; cottages

pentre/pentref -i   village

pentrefan	hamlet
penty -au	cottage; hut
perfed(d) -au -i -ion	heartland; interior
perllan -nau -noedd	orchard
pert	pretty
perth -i	hedge; bush
perthen	bush
petrisen	partridge
pi or pia	magpie
pica	sharp; pointed
pig -au	point
pîl	tidal creek; tidal pool
Pile	from Welsh: Y Pîl = creek
Pill	from English: pill (Welsh pil = creek)
piod	magpie
pioden	magpie(s)
piogen	magpie

pistyll -oedd	spout; well
plas -au	mansion; open space
plwmp	pump
plwyf -i -ydd	parish
Plynlimon	from Welsh: Pumlumon (?five hills, ?five chimneys)
poeth	warm; hot; burnt
ponc -iau	hillock
pont -ydd	bridge; arch over. The name of the river bridged, or of a person usually follows
Pont Neath Vaughan	English version of Welsh: Pontneddfechan
Pontyates	English version of Welsh: Pont-iets
Pontypool	a Welsh/English mix: English pool here means the river (Llwyd)
Pontypridd	corruption of Pont y tŷ pridd
poplysen	poplar
porfa/porfeydd (pl)	grazing for cattle
porth (1) -oedd	gap; pass; gate (of town)
porth (2) -au -oedd	port; harbour; ferry; landing place
Porthcawl	cawl comes from the English: (sea) kale
Powys	tribal land in medieval Wales (Latin: *pagenses*)
praidd	flock
preiddiau	flocks
pren -nau	tree
Prestatyn	from English: prest=priest + tun =farm, or house
priciau	kindling
pridd -oedd	soil; earth
prif	chief
prydferth	beautiful
prys	a person's name: Price
prysg -au	copse
pum or pump	five
pwll -yn -au	pool; pit (including mining)
pydew	pools; pits (including mining)
Pyle	from Welsh: pîl
pyll	tidal pools; tidal creeks
pyllan	pools; pits (including mining)

pyr	short; also a person's name
pyrth	harbours; ferries; ports
pysgod or pysgodin or pysg	fish

Q

There is no **Q** in the Welsh alphabet.

R

ran -nau	piece; part
Resolven	from Welsh: rhos + soflen (stubble)
rhaeadr -au	waterfall
rhan -nau	piece
Rhayader	from Welsh: Rhaeadr Gwy (waterfall on the river Wye)
rhedyn	fern
rheidol	a river name
rheol or rhewl	the road
rhew	frost; ice
rhiangoll	a river name
rhic	gap; pass
rhidian	a person's name
rhig (1)	gap; pass
rhig (2)	heather
rhingyll -iaid	bailiff, i.e. an official with judicial powers
rhiw -iau	hill; slope; ascent
Rhondda	from Welsh: Glyn yr Hoddni (river); then yr Hoddni was corrupted via rhoddni to rhondda
Rhoose	from Welsh: rhos
rhos (1) -ydd	upland; moor; heath; down
rhos (2)	roses
rhosan	a river name
rhosfa	mountain pasture
rhosyn	rose
rhudd	red; crimson
rhufeinig	Roman
Rhuthin or Rhuthun	from Welsh: rhudd + din = red fort

rhyd -au   river crossing; ford

Rhydderch   a person's name: Roderick
rhyg   rye
Rhymney   a river name
rhyn   point; head of
rhys   a person's name: Rees
rida   a person's name: Fryda
ro   pebbly
Roath   perhaps from Irish *rath* = fort
roc   rock
Rockfield   from Norman French: *Roche*=rock + *ville*
                   =town
ru   slope; ascent, from rhic

S

saeson   english
saeth -au   arrow; also a river name
saffrwn   crocus
safn   mouth
saint   saints
sais   englishman
saith   a river name
sangen   a person's name

sant -iau   saint

santes   female saint
sarn -au   causeway
Saron   Biblical name
sawdde   a river name
sawel   a person's name
Sblot (Y)   from English: plot (of land)
sedd -a   seat
sefin   a person's name
seint   saints
Seion   Biblical name: Zion
seisnig   relating to the English
seisyll   a person's name
seisyllwg   land ruled by Seisyll = Sersyll
senghen(n)   a person's name: Sangan or Sangen

sêr/seren	stars/star
seri	causeway
serth	steep
sewyl	a person's name
sgebion	bishop
shôn	a person's name: John
sialc -au	chalk
sigl(o)	shaking; rocking
siglen -nydd	bog
sili	a person's name: Sully
silian	a person's name
silio	a saint's name: Sulio
silwy	a tribal name
siôn	a person's name: John
sioni	a person's name: John
sionyn	a person's name: John
siôr	a person's name: George
siorys	a person's name: George
sir -oedd	shire; county
siriol	bright; pleasant
Skenfrith	English version of Ynys Gynwraidd
Sketty or Sgeti	from Welsh: Ynys + Geti
Snowdonia	pure English (Snowdonia in Welsh is Eryri)
soch	a river name
Soe	a saint's name: Soe or Tysoe
soflen	stubble
Splot	from English: plot (of land)
staffan	a saint's name: Steven
stâl -au	stall
stalwyn	stallion
steffan	a saint's name: Steven
sul or sulio	a person's name: Sulio
Swansea	Swedish viking: Swayne's island
sŵn	sound; noise
swydd -au -i	district; county
sych -ion	dry
symlog	wild strawberies
syth	straight

T

taf	very big; a river name
tafarn -au	tavern
taff	a river name, from Taf
tafol	dock (the plant)
tai (but care with tair)	houses
tair (but care with tai)	three
tâl	front; end
talar	from tâl + ardd, or tâl + ar (l)
taleisin	a person's name: Taliesin
talfainc	throne
taliesin	a person's name
Talley	from Welsh: Talyllychau
talog	a person's name
tan (l)	under; below
tân (2)	fire
tanad	shining; also a river name
tanat	a river name; see tanad just above
tanglwys	a person's name
tap	ledge
tarnau	a person's name: Teyrnon
tarren -ydd	(rocky) knoll
tarw	bull
tawe	a river name
teap	step; sharp rise in ground
teg	fair; beautiful
tegan	a person's name
tegeingl	from Latin: the *Deceangli* tribe
tegfedd	a saint's name
tegid	a person's name: Tacitus
tegyr	a person's name
teifi	a river name
teilo	a saint's name
teirw	bulls
telerch	a person's name
teliad	comely
telyn	harp
tenau	thin
Tenby	from Welsh: Dinbych, from din + bychan
tenni	a person's name

terfyn -au	boundary
teulwyddog	a saint's name
tew	thick
teyrnon	a person's name
thafarn	tavern
thegla	a person's name
tillery	a river name, perhaps after Tyleri
tin	base; tail
Tintern	English version of Welsh: Din + Dwrn (possibly a person's name)
tir -oedd	land
tirion	kindly
titw	tit (bird)
tlws	beautiful; pretty
tomen -ydd	motte; heap; mound
tomos	a person's name: Thomas
ton -nau (1)	lay lands – poor, unploughed land or once arable land left to go to grass
ton -nau (2)	wave
tonna	plural of ton (1) above
top	top
torlan -nau	river bank
Towy	Welsh: Tywi, a river name
towyn	sandy beach
traed (1)	at the feet/bases of
traed (2)	feet (personal)
traeth -au	beach
trallong	marsh
trallwm	marsh
trap	step
trapp	?step ?rising ground
traws	across; towards
tre or **tref**	originally a homestead; home; farm. Later, in Middle Ages, a town (often followed by a person's name)
Trecastle	from Welsh: tre + castell
Trefor	from Welsh tre + fawr
treharn	a person's name
tri	three

trigfa or trigfan	dwelling place
trin -oedd	battle
tro	turn; twist
trobwll	whirlpool
troddi	strong river
troed	foot of; base
tros	across; over
trum -iaf -io	crest; ridge
truman	small ridge
trydedd	third (ordinal)
trydydd	third (ordinal)
tryfan	rounded or pointed peak
trywerin	a river name
tudful	a person's name
tudno	a person's name
tudur	a person's name: Tudor
tudwal	a person's name
tudweil	a person's name: Tudwal
tutglyd	a person's name
twlc	sty
twlch	hut; cottage
twll	hole
twm	a person's name: Thomas
twmpath	tump; mound
twr	heap
twˆr	tower
twrch	boar
twrog	a person's name
twym	warm
twymyn	a river name
twyn	hillock
twyncyn	a person's name: Tomkins
tŷ (1) or ty (1)	house; in South Wales it can often mean a church of the named saint
tŷ (2) or ty (2)	if tŷ or ty (in one of its derived forms dy or dŷ or de) comes after the word llan and immediately before a saint's name, it signifies a high level of (religious) respect, implying something like 'most holy', perhaps

tybiau	a saint's name
tydfil	a person's name: Tudful
tyfodwg	a saint's name
tyla -u	hillside; ascent
tylcau	sties
tyle	hills; ascents
tyleri	a person's name
tyllau	holes
tylluan -od	owl
tyn	homestead; small farm
ty'n	the house in; in South Wales could mean the church in
tyno	dale; hollows
tyrau	towers
tyrchod	boars
tysul	a person's name
tywod	sand
tywyll	dark
tywyn -au	sea shore
tywynnog	a saint's name
tywysog -ion	prince

U

uan	a saint's name: Buan
uchaf	highest
uchder	height
uchedydd	skylark
uchel	high
uchelder -au	height
uchelwydd	mistletoe
ucho or uchod	above
udd -ydd	lord
ugre	a person's name
ulw	ashes
un	one
unben	nobleman
unfed	first
us	chaff
Usk	Welsh: Wysg (sometimes Wy); a river name
uwch (1)	above
uwch (2)	can mean that side, their side (compare with is (2)

V

There is no **V** in Welsh, but there are a few place-names, via English corruptions, mainly.

Vardre	a bonded village under the authority of a steward, from faerdre
Vetherine	from Welsh: Bwytherin
Vyrnwy	from Welsh: Efyrnwy

W

wal -iau	wall
walch	hawk
wastad	flat
wasted or wastod	flat land
waun	moor
wawr	dawn
well	better; superior
wellte	a person's name: Melltan, or Mellte
wen	fair; beautiful; white. Also a river name
wenarth	a person's name: Gwenarth
went	field; plain; market venue
Wentloog	from Welsh: Gwynllwg (a person's name)
wenvoe	from gwen + fo(el)
werful	a person's name: Gwerful
wern	marsh; alder trees
weunydd	moors
wiail	rods; switches
wialen	rod; twig
wiber	viper
wig -oedd	wood
willim	a person's name: Gwylim, William
wiwer	red squirrel
wlad	district
wladus	a person's name: Gwladus
wnion	a river name
wnnog	a saint's name: Tywynnog
wnog	a river name
wrda	a person's name: Gwrda(f)
wrin	a person's name: Gwrin
wrog	a person's name: Twrog
wr	worker

wrw	a person's name
wy (at the end of a tribal name)	gives the name of their lands e.g. Oethwy, Aethwy
wybren	skylark
wyddel(an)	a person's name: Gwyddel(an)
wyddfa	tumulus, grave; also uncultivated upland
Wye (river)	Welsh: Gwy
Wylan	a person's name: Gwylan
wyll	owl
wyllt	wild
ŵyn	lambs
wynne	white; shining
wynt	wind
wynwyn	onions
Wysg	from the first part of Latin name of the Roman 2nd legion (*Isca Augusta*)
wythan	a person's name: Gwythan

X

There is no **X** in the Welsh alphabet.

Y

y	the, but also see linked Key Words **yn**, **ym**, **yng** and **yr**, below
ych -ain -en	ox
yd -au	corn
ydd (after a name)	shows possession of lands etc. e.g. Meirionydd = lands of Meirion
ydfa	fruitful
ydfran	rook
ym	in; at; into; for
ymhell	afar
ymyl -on	edge; margin
yn (1)	in; at; into; for
yn (2)	at ends of words implies small
ynn	ash trees

yng   in; at; into; for

    ynog   ?bees
    ynolwyn   a person's name: Gynolwyn or Gwenolwyn
    ynys -oedd   riverside meadow; island
    Ynyston   English: East tun (town)

yr   the; of the

    ysbyty   hospital; hospice
    ysgall   thistle
    ysgaw/ysgawen   elder trees/elder tree
    ysgeib   bishop
    ysgir   a river name: Esgair
    ysgob   bishop
    ysgor   elder
    ysgub -au   sheaf; broom (brush)
    ysgubor -iau   barn
    ysguthan   woodpigeon
    ysgyfarnog -od   hare
    ystad (1)   furlong (about 200 metres)
    ystâd (2)/ystadau   estate/estates
    ystal   stall (animals)
    ystlum -od   bat (animal)
    ystlus -au   flank
    ystrad -au   vale; broad valley; flat bottom
    ystum -iau   a bend
    ystwyth   winding; a river name
    yw   yew
    ywel   a person's name: Howell or Hywel
    ywen   yew

Z

There is no **Z** in the Welsh alphabet.

**– Wales within your reach:
an attractive series
at attractive prices!**

1. Welsh Talk
Heini Gruffudd
086243 447 5
£2.95

2. Welsh Dishes
Rhian Williams
086243 492 0
£2.95

3. Welsh Songs
Lefi Gruffudd (ed.)
086243 525 0
£3.95

4. Welsh Mountain Walks
Dafydd Andrews
086243 547 1
£3.95

5. Welsh Organic Recipes
Dave and Barbara Frost
086243 574 9
£3.95

6. Welsh Railways
Jim Green
086243 551 X
£3.95

7. Welsh Place Names
Brian Davies
086243 514 5
£3.95

8. Welsh Castles
Geraint Roberts
086243 550 1
£3.95

9. Welsh Rugby Heroes
Androw Bennett
086243 552 8
£3.95

Also to be published in the *It's Wales* series:

Welsh National Heroes

Welsh History

Welsh Jokes

The *It's Wales* series
is just one of a wide range
Welsh interest publications
from Y Lolfa.
For a full list of books currently in print,
send now for your free copy
of our new, full-colour Catalogue
– or simply surf into our website
at **www.ylolfa.com.**

Talybont Ceredigion Cymru/*Wales* SY24 5AP
ffôn 0044 (0)1970 832 304 *ffacs* 832 782 *isdn* 832 813
e-bost ylolfa@ylolfa.com *y we* www.ylolfa.com